ABERDEEN GREATS

ABERDEEN GREATS

ALASTAIR GUTHRIE

SPORTSPRINT PUBLISHING
EDINBURGH

ISBN 0 85976 278 5

My sincere thanks must go to the Aberdeen FC players,
past and present, who made writing this book such a pleasure;
and to the Library Department of Aberdeen Journals Ltd
for their willing co-operation in providing illustrations.

Phototypeset by Beecee Typesetting Services
Printed in Great Britain by Bell & Bain Ltd., Glasgow

Foreword by Buff Hardie, of Scotland the What?

Far's the paper?

Hiv' ye finished yer book?

Aye. I enjoyed it. Div' ye want tae read it? Ye can ha'e a shottie if ye like.

Let's see. Nine greats by Alastair Guthrie. Nine great Aiberdeen players — nine? Is 'at a' the great Aiberdeen players he could think o'? Or is it aboot the nine greatest Aiberdeen players?

Neither, Bunty. It's just nine great players a' fae different periods since the war. If he'd included a' the greats that hiv' every played for Aiberdeen the book would hiv' finished up like *War an' Peace.* Mind you, it still must hiv' been difficult pickin' his nine. There's been sae mony great players played for Aiberdeen.

Aye. There wis Willie Lennie.

First Aiberdeen player tae be capped.

Mind? He hid a shoppie in Hilton Road fan we wis little. There wis Frank Dunlop.

He went on tae be the artistic director o' the Edinburgh Festival, Bunty.

I'm nae surprised. I even got a slow foxtrot fae him at the Beach Ballroom. He wis a rare dancer.

Tommy Pearson, Charlie Cooke, Zoltan Varga.

Wis he fae Hilton?

Fred Martin, Archie Baird, Alex McLeish — the list is endless, Bunty. They couldna a' get in the book. But I'll tell ye fa could easy hiv' been in. Me.

You? You never played for the Dons.

No. But it was aye my ambition to play for them. An' it could so easily hiv' happened, Bunty.

Fit ye haverin' aboot?

Nae long efter the war, fan I wis assistant trainer for Parkvale, I wis in cherge o' the magic sponge — weel it wis my Ma's dish-cloth actually — an' the lemonade bottle full o' water at the match at Central Park. Davie Halliday, the Dons manager, hid beed at the picters at the Astoria an' fan he cam' oot he watched the last 10 minutes o' the game, durin' which I his tae attend tae twa o' oor players that hid collided wi' een anither runnin' up tae the ref tae dispute a throw-in. Weel, Davie Halliday wis that impressed he asked if I'd be interested in a job on the ground staff at Pittodrie.

I've never heard this story afore.

I could never bring mysel' tae tell ye, Bunty. 'Cos it's the saddest story o' my life. I hid tae say No, 'cos the next wik I wis gain' awa tae start my National service an' by the time I cam' oot twa years later they'd got somebody.

But even if ye'd been able tae tak' the job ye still widna hiv' played for the Dons.

Bunty, if I'd jist got inta Pittodrie, if I'd got my toes on the lowest rung o' the ladder, there's nae sayin' fit I could hiv' achieved. You ken fit I'm like — iron will, rugged determination, rigorous self-discipline. I wid hiv' snatched my chance tae stand in for somebody — George Hamilton, or somebody like 'at — in a practice game. I wid hiv' made an impact. I wid hiv' stuck in and I wid hiv' become a star. Dinna shak' yer heid, Bunty. I wid hiv' been the spik o' a' the pubs in Aiberdeen. Old men who had seen them all — Alex Jackson, Donald Colman, yea, even unto Willie Lennie himsel' — wid hiv' sung my praises an' jostled een anither tae touch the hem o' my bicycle cape.

But it wisna tae be. A tragic story, Dod.

Aye. I never did play for the Dons. If I hid, I could hiv' been a great.

Weel, ye'll just need tae find some ither wye o' gettin' inta Alastair Guthrie's book.

Contents

The return from Sweden with the European prize sparked off the biggest street party Aberdeen has ever witnessed as 100,000 celebrated.

CHAPTER ONE

Introduction

It wasn't so much a case of knowing where to start, but realising when to stop. For, honestly, there are so many players who could — and possibly should — have rightly featured alongside my nine-man team that a sequel — Aberdeen Greats II — might be required on bookshelves.

But the nine players I have deliberately chosen in the years stemming from the Second World War capture the essence, spirit and drive of the Dons through all their major achievements.

From George Hamilton and Archie Glen, who were instrumental in helping Aberdeen create a winning mould, to the likes of Willie Miller, Jim Leighton ,and Gordon Strachan, who reached those dizzy European heights in Gothenburg. And the trio's medal-collecting didn't stop in Sweden.

In between, Graham Leggat, Martin Buchan, Bobby Clark and Joe Harper made sure Aberdeen gathered in some silver.

But this isn't a chronicle of cup finals and flag days. The Greats also tell of their feelings for team-mates, managers, contemporaries and both on and off-field situations.

Football is a game of deep emotions and many feel it has a fickle old way of kicking players in the teeth when they're on a high. But the opposite can be said of keeper Bobby Clark.

The deeply-hurt Don was at an all-time low after the Scotland defence conceded five embarrassing goals to the English that night it all went wrong in the 1973 Centenary International at a frosty, horrible Hampden.

'I came in for criticism, along with other members of the

Super heroes. The delighted Dons gather round the European Super Cup after humbling Hamburg.

defence. Even after a few days the defeat was still painful and I was beginning to wonder if I would ever smile again.

'Then I received a letter with a Manchester postmark. On opening it I found a little printed plastic disc which bore the legend, 'Come in number one. Your time is up! Yours in jest, Martyr Buchan.'

Clark's former Aberdeen colleague, Old Trafford captain Martin Buchan, had also been pilloried for his part in the five-goal defeat. But his dry and clever sense of humour lifted his wounded old team-mate out of a depression.

Then the ever-chirpy, flame-haired Gordon Strachan had a direct way of raising a laugh.

The heroes of Gothenburg begin to realise they really have won the European Cup-Winners' Cup.

In 1980 Strachan followed 1971 winner Buchan into the hall of fame as the Scottish Football Writers' Player of the Year. Willie Miller was also to receive the honour in 1984.

Wee Gordon took his place at the top table at the annual dinner and belied any outward signs of nervousness when he opened his acceptance speech with, 'First of all I would like to thank my manager, Alex Ferguson, for his part in getting me here tonight. He drove the car from Aberdeen.'

Eddie Turnbull, a coach and technician ahead of his time, also had a personal way of handling incidents.

One Sunday evening the Dons boss was settling down in his Aberdeen home to relax in front of the TV before concentrating on a midweek European tie at Pittodrie. But his night's peace was disturbed by the unexpected arrival of Joe Harper.

Union Street, Aberdeen, was to be a familiar route for the open-deck bus and the Scottish Cup.

And the news Harper had brought would have put most managers off the prospect of a tough European game. But not the unique Turnbull.

Harper had raised his clothing to reveal a flesh gash in his back following a disagreement with a door. Eight stitches had been inserted and it appeared as though the Dons would be without their master marksman.

Turnbull remained forthright, 'It doesn't matter about the stitches because you're still playing.' Play Harper did . . . and score.

It was Turnbull who gave the Dons back respectability and presence with Scottish Cup success. He also shook Scottish football to the core with his innovation and advances. The game was more than just selecting a regular 2-3-5 formation every Saturday.

'I was coaching Queen's Park when I was asked if I would

No danger of the Scottish Cup being allowed to slip in this 1984 parade as it is in the firm grip of keeper Jim Leighton. Joining him in the front row are fellow greats, Gordon Strachan and Willie Miller.

be interested in the job at Aberdeen. Naturally, the answer was yes.

'I came up to Aberdeen on the Sunday to be interviewed with a few others and I was told to return about tea-time. When I did I was given the chance.

'But I couldn't believe it, because the place was a shambles. I had previously been with Hibs, who were the best club in the game at that time.

'I was used to the best and to success and that's what I wanted to give Aberdeen. So I really modelled the club on what I had learned during my years at Easter Road.

'It was difficult because I was fielding a side of kids who hadn't fully realised their potential. We won the Scottish Cup and finished second in the league.

'To go to some place such as Celtic Park and win in

those days was no mean feat. We did it and beat them in the cup final. I was very proud of the lads in that side. It was a European team.

'They were still learning and I don't know how good they could have become. No-one can visualise where they might have finished up. We were doing things in training and on the park in the late 1960s and early 1970s that they're doing today.

'They were a forward-thinking side who were always encouraged to do just that. Players are restricted too much in modern football and not really allowed to express themselves.

'There's a fear of losing . . . and that doesn't suit the fans. The paying spectators want goalmouth incidents for their money.

'I've been always a great believer that a team must have a winger. There's nothing better than watching a natural winger making his way to the byeline and getting a telling cross over or a cut-back in. All the really good sides carry a winger.'

Turnbull was already committed to this theory in that 1970 triumph over Celtic. He took the bold step of blooding 17-year-old left-winger Arthur Graham in his first Scottish Cup-tie. And Bumper left the old stadium clutching a winner's medal.

There's a strong mutual respect between the man who had the vision and those who had the ability to carry out his orders once they were away from the confines of the dressing-room. Eddie did have a way with them.

Bobby Clark, for instance, was not only taken under his wing, but Turnbull also initially threw open his home door and laid on lodgings for the fledgling keeper when he followed him to the North-east from Hampden.

And for those who had been signed from hungrier, less privileged backgrounds, Turnbull made them feel like kings by insisting they were taken to a top tailor and decked out from head to toe. Only in the best, you understand.

Manager Alex Ferguson holds high the familiar Scottish Cup in 1986. It was the last trophy he won and the final parade he took part in before departing for Manchester United.

Turnbull had the necessary experience and the iron character to cajole his players and to win over the fans . . . eventually.

When the Pittodrie crowd of 13,000 felt they had been short-changed for a meagre 2-1 Scottish Cup win over Second Division Clydebank on Wednesday, February 11, 1970, they gave vent to their feelings by jeering Turnbull and his team all the way to the dressing-room.

Two months later those same supporters freely gave Turnbull joyous and continuous choruses of 'Happy Birthday to You' throughout the length and breadth of the celebrating city. The Dons were parading the cup for the first time in 23 years.

Parades, of course, followed with Ally MacLeod at the Pittodrie bow and were a steady feature under Alex Ferguson's golden eight-year reign.

Such was the expectancy under the fiery Ferguson that the Red Army ventured to finals convinced that the trophies would automatically return with them to Pittodrie. It wasn't a case of if, but when.

Players and managers took the public bows and credit. But there was another team working just as hard behind the scenes out of the glare of the fans.

For the progressive Dons board, particularly under the astute guidance of chairman Dick Donald and the late vice-chairman Chris Anderson, let British football see where it should be going in terms of safety and comfort by reshaping Pittodrie into a model for the others to follow.

The stadium became the first to provide a seat for each fan. And there is a roof to cover every head, too.

But there has been one man, always happy to remain well in the background, who was on the staff when that first title came along in 1955 and was still doing his diligent duties as club trainer when he celebrated his 60th birthday in 1989 — Teddy Scott.

Modest Teddy would shun any praise or plaudits for grooming young hopefuls into players, or for making sure hampers were always organised.

Quiet-spoken Scott, appointed to the coaching side in 1958, did make a slight error once just to show he was human. It only served to underline his importance.

Aberdeen embarked on the long road to Gothenburg by having to fulfil a preliminary round of the Cup-Winners' Cup in picturesque Switzerland against Sion.

But when the Dons arrived in the Alps at one of the most breathtakingly beautiful grounds in Europe it was discovered that Teddy had packed the wrong colour of socks.

Boss. Ferguson joked to the assembled dressing-room squad that it would mean instant dismissal for Scott. It was the lazer-witted Strachan who shot right back with, 'That'll mean there are nine jobs going at Pittodrie, then.'

It's said that no-one is indispensable. At Pittodrie, Teddy Scott could lodge a strong case against that claim.

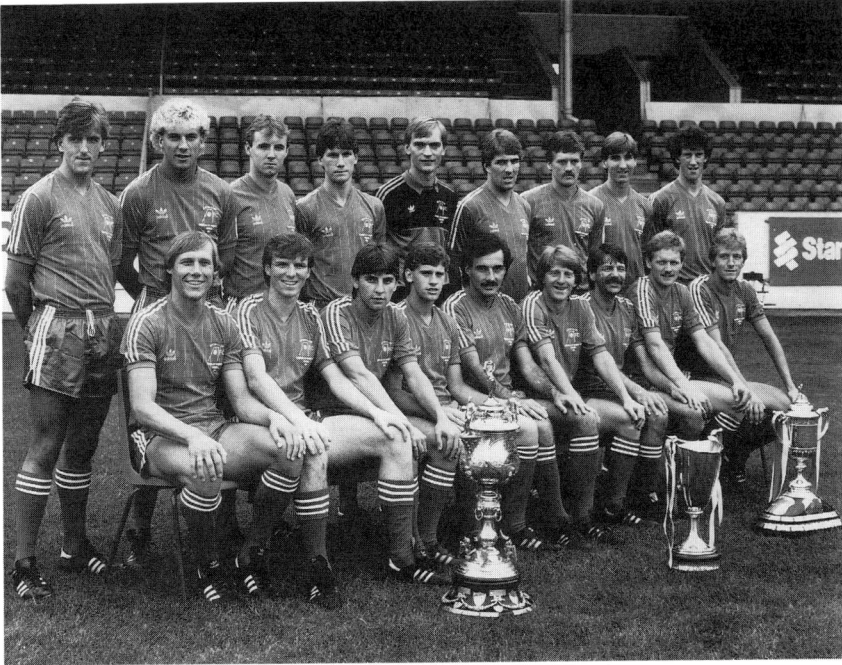

The European Cup-Winners' Cup is flanked by the Aberdeenshire Cup and the Scottish Cup as the Dons squad show off their haul for season 1982/83.

That wonderfully alert full-back Stuart Kennedy, robbed of several years because of injury and who will persistently challenge me as to why he wasn't given a full chapter, felt the draught without Teddy.

'I was left in interim charge of the reserves after Teddy had gone along with the first team after Archie Knox left for Dundee. You think there's nothing to it when it comes to seeing to players' needs.

'But when the hamper arrived in the dressing-room I just looked to the heavens and cried, "Teddy, where are you now?"

'Hampers are taken for granted with Teddy around. Without him it's pandemonium. He's a whole team wrapped into one . . . and that's not even mentioning his coaching ability.'

No wonder stars such as Kennedy, Strachan, Buchan, McLeish, Miller and many, many more reverently refer to him as That Great Man of Pittodrie.

A succession of managers have benefited from Teddy's advice and none more so than one who asked him to keep a close watch on a particular youngster.

He's not doing enough in training, Teddy was informed. But the experienced Scott eye saw it differently. And it's just as well as the player in question was none other than the club's most successful skipper, Willie Miller.

There are fans who must have compiled their own private lists of greats, and I probably wouldn't argue over their selections.

A start could have been made back in 1907 only four years after the Aberdeen FC we know today came into being. Charlie O'Hagen, the Dons inside-left who had been bought for £175 from Middlesborough, turned out for his native Nothern Ireland against England in February that year to become the club's first international.

Then the following year Willie Lennie, left wing to O'Hagen, was the first Don to be honoured by Scotland. And he crowned the debut against Wales at Dens Park by scoring in a 2-1 victory before a 15,000 crowd.

Another great Don, Alex Cheyne, was said to be the man responsible for unleashing the Hampden roar on April 13, 1929. Scotland and England were locked at 0-0 until inside-right Cheyne found the thunder in the voices of the 110,512 by scoring the only goal direct from a corner.

Benny Yorston, whose only cap came in a goalless draw with Northern Ireland in Belfast in 1931, would be a priceless commodity today. The Nigg-born centre-forward stood at barely 5ft 5in, but he could take a goal with either foot or in the air. Even King Joey couldn't crack the 38 league goals Benny grabbed in season 1929/30.

Others, of course, followed throughout the years . . . Donald Colman, Matt Armstrong, Willie Mills, Willie Cooper, Jack Allister, Alex Young, Archie Baird, Harry Yorston, Fred Martin, Billy Little, Tubby Ogston, Willie Young, Jinky Smith.

And there would be those who may well argue with a degree of conviction that it would be absurd not to feature Charlie Cooke or Zoltan Varga all on their own.

Cooke the artiste was a rare player purists purred over. Many would have willingly crawled over broken glass to take in his finest displays. And the Hungarian with the wanderlust in his veins, Varga, is generally regarded as the most naturally gifted player ever to have completed just 31 league and cup matches for the Dons.

Pittodrie fans weaned on the abundances of the 1980s would insist strongly that Alex McLeish, Eric Black, Neale Cooper, Neil Simpson, John Hewitt, Stewart McKimmie and Charlie Nicholas have been overlooked.

No-one was overlooked. And to all those marvellous Pittodrie players who have thrilled thousands but failed to make my first nine, I'm sorry. But you can only send out one side at a time.

CHAPTER TWO

George Hamilton

George Hamilton was a gentleman in the ruthless world of goal scorers. So it wasn't long at all before he was awarded the title of Aberdeen's own Gentleman George. It was in keeping with his outwardly placid nature and appropriate right from the minute he began his career as a Don just before the outbreak of the Second World War.

There was, however, one minor blemish — a booking! — before he called it a day in 1955. But George maintains it certainly wasn't justified. 'I enjoyed my football and always felt that if it was worth playing, it was worth playing well and fairly. I was only booked once during my career and it wasn't even for dirty play.

'It came during a League Cup marathon with Hibs in 1950. We had beaten them 4-1 in the first leg and I had managed to score. Incredibly, we then lost the second game by the same score and went on to a replay at Ibrox, which finished all square at 1-1. Then, to crown it all, we lost 5-1 at Hampden.

'But during that extra half-hour at Ibrox one of our players was penalised for next to nothing and I just happened to say, "That wasn't a foul, ref." Next minute my name went into J. Jackson's wee black book. Considering the way some modern players back-chat referees and seem to intimidate them I feel I was hard done by. The booking surprised manager Dave Halliday just as much as it did me, but you know you're not supposed to talk back to referees and that's that.

'Dissent is a bookable offence, and rightly so, but maybe referees concern themselves too much with petty incidents. Swearing is an example and I don't believe a

The master class of 1947 who brought the Scottish Cup to Pittodrie. Back row — McLaughlin, Cooper, McKenna, Johnstone, Waddell, Taylor, Dunlop. Front — Harris, Hamilton, Williams, Baird, McCall.

player should be booked for swearing, provided he takes heed of a telling-off. It's understandable when a player swears out of frustration.

'There are also players who get into trouble with referees for just being hard players. Some people may forget that football is a physical game and it's a game for men. But there are players who should be punished and punished severely. These are the type who go out to deliberately injure an opponent by tackling with their studs up or by going over the ball.'

Hamilton made his way to Pittodrie from Queen of the South during the close season in 1937, and even his record £3000 transfer fee must be regarded as one of the best bargains of all time. Yet the football-daft young Hamilton doubted if he was good enough for the Irvine Academy team, never mind a top professional outfit.

'My father died when I was 10, so everyone had to pull their weight. I worked as a butcher's boy and would slip away on Saturday afternoons to watch Irvine Meadow at home. I don't think I saw myself as a professional player, as I struggled to get into the school side. I don't believe I was destined to scale any academic heights, and when I was included in the school side I was as happy as a sandboy in the Sahara. Then it was on to Boys' Brigade football with the 1st Irvine Co. and I used to hang about after meetings on a Friday night to see if I'd been chosen for the team the next day.

'When you consider just how much money there is around in the game today it seems plain daft to consider that one of my happiest moments came when I actually signed for Irvine Meadow. I was given a 10 shilling note (that's 50p today) as a signing-on fee. To my mother Elizabeth and sister Jean that was a lot of money and I couldn't scarper home quickly enough to hand over the cash.

'A year later and I was on my way to Queen of the South. There had been one other club interested — Rangers. I had just had my tonsils taken out when I received an invitation from manager Bill Struth to become a guest Ranger. That was a real tonic and I actually played two trials for the Gers before Struth — a brusque but fair man — decided against offering me signing terms. The opinion was that I was too light and just too small for senior football.

'Rangers were entitled to their opinion, but Billy Halliday, brother of Aberdeen manager Dave, didn't agree and he had been impressed at the way I had performed at Palmerston Park. Even at that, it came as something of a shock when I was instructed to report to the ground and I believed it was for no more than a round of re-signing talks. But Dave Halliday had travelled down from Pittodrie to try to sign me. I agreed straight away.'

That significant acquisition took place on May 4, 1938, and the £3000 fee doubled the Dons' previous best! Only 24 days later Hammy was pitched straight into the first team at inside-right for an Ibrox date with English king-pins Chelsea in the Empire Exhibition tournament. He scored in a 4-0 cruise against the English side. Hammy was on his way and even finished the season as Pittodrie's leading scorer with 19 goals.

'Halliday was the manager, but it was Donald Colman — the man who gave the game the dug-out — who took training. It was very hard and few players developed into big-heads when Donald was around. But it was a novelty if we got the ball to work with — and we weren't allowed on to the pitch for a practice match. The groundsman didn't approve of his pitch being used in between competitive matches. And with no alternative pitches in the area it was small wonder we became a little rusty from time to time.'

But as Hamilton began his march, so too did Herr Hitler by stomping all over Europe. Arguably, the very best of Hamilton was lost during those war-torn years. Hamilton was simply happy to return from active service. Several colleagues didn't. 'I was once on a troopship which had to call in at Gibraltar for repairs. The rest of the convoy continued on their way and the German submarines were waiting for them. We lost a lot of lads and I lost two good friends. I've been asked if I was ever bitter over the fact that the Second World War maybe coincided with my peak playing days. But I never saw it that way at all. I came back. Many didn't.

'Coaching methods, tactics and preparations were far removed from today's teachings. I've often wondered just how we managed to get by with what we did. Still, I'm not yet totally convinced that all the modern techniques are good for a player and maybe they just sometimes stifle a lad's ability. But Dave Halliday did produce a blackboard once a week and we were shown exactly how opponents would be beaten and how we would score many goals on the Saturday.

'On match days at Pittodrie it was a case of a meal in Aberdeen's Caledonian Hotel and a discussion covering our last game and the one only an hour or so away before we set out to walk to the stadium. I don't believe it would be advisable for the Dons to take a stroll down Union Street and onto Pittodrie today. Some fans could be awkward, you know. But we were never approached by any rival supporters and the fact we were on our way to play seemed to please those who joined us in the walk. Anyway, I thought it was a good thing.'

One self-admitted blunder Hammy did make was at the tail-end of 1947 when he asked away from Aberdeen, although he had no specific quarrel with the club. He took his boots to Tynecastle in a swap involving Archie Kelly — and was swiftly back again only six months later in a £10,000 deal. 'I went to Edinburgh by train for talks with Hearts and on the way I was still swithering over what was the right thing to do. Now I know it was one of the daftest things I did by believing I would be bettering myself by joining Hearts. From the moment the transfer was suggested I wasn't sure in my own mind if I should go. Dave Halliday was willing to keep me and there was a place for me with the Dons.

'But I decided to make the move to Hearts. And it was definitely one of the biggest mistakes of my life. Hearts manager Dave McLean had conducted the transfer by the book and I had nothing at all against the man. But Hearts at that point were a side struggling against relegation and it just didn't work out for me at Tynecastle. There was also the added pressure of having to fulfil a full 12-hour day just to train in Edinburgh. I left Irvine at 7.00 each morning to be able to report for a 9.45 am start at Tynecastle and it was always well after 7.00 pm before I got back home. It was a hard day's work and it didn't take too long to realise I had made a major blunder by leaving the Dons.'

Hamilton went sailing back to Pittodrie in the summer of 1948 from the middle of the Irish Sea. 'I had been selected for a representative match in Dublin and I was hanging over the ship's rail during the crossing watching the sea flowing by and wondering where my career was going. Then Aberdeen director John Robbie appeared at my

It's the goal which put the Dons on their way to that first Scottish Cup triumph in 1947. Billy McCall turns to acclaim George's header, which left Hibs keeper Jimmy Kerr helpless.

elbow and during our conversation he inquired how I was getting on with Hearts and went on to deliver the words I wanted to hear most 'How would you like to come back to Pittodrie?' I think he knew what my answer would be well in advance. He kept me on tenterhooks for a bit by saying he would see what he could do. But the clubs must have already opened talks before this approach. Anyway, I had no hesitation in making my way back to the Granite City. Aberdeen was the only place for me. I should have realised that fact all along.'

Gentleman George's career was not without its moments of high drama and deep controversy on and off the pitch. There came a flashpoint in 1952 when Hammy had a four-week club suspension slapped on him for refusing to turn out against Rangers. To this day, Hamilton is adamant he was given the rawest of deals from the Dons.

'Manager Halliday accused me of being a shirker. But I'll

let the facts speak for themselves. In my long association with the Dons I never gave less than 100% in any game. Even those few brief months with Hearts didn't alter my attitude and I was always keen and proud to wear an Aberdeen jersey. The truth of the matter is that I just wasn't in any physical or mental state to tackle Rangers in a League Cup-tie at Ibrox on Saturday, August 16, 1952. Many years have now gone by since that one-month suspension without pay and my opinion hasn't altered. I was badly done by.

'I had been called up for what was termed Z Service. After a spell in the Royal Engineers, where I was a PE sergeant, I had to return to Aldershot for further duty. This, I might say, was nothing out of the ordinary in the years following the war. I had been involved in arduous work at Aldershot for a fortnight when I was told I would have to travel overnight to Glasgow for the cup-tie against Rangers. Roy Henderson, the Queen of the South goal-keeper, was also on a similar course at Aldershot and he, too, was on his way back to Scotland for a match.

'We both went to the left luggage office to collect our kits and then we parted ways on the train. I was amazed when Roy went off to a specially-booked sleeper and I was expected to sit for the next 12 hours or so in a compartment. Sleep was out of the question and there was even great difficulty in getting to the toilet during this most unpleasant journey out of England. When I arrived at Queen Street Station, Glasgow, I knew I was in no condition to tackle a game within a few hours.

'I made my way to the team's hotel suffering badly from train-lag and clear that I wasn't fit to play. More fit to drop. Playing that afternoon would have been unfair and unjust to the rest of the team. Even after a wash and a filling breakfast, the exhaustion wasn't out of my body. It grew worse when I knew I was earmarked to play a demanding right-half role in a crucial game. Aberdeen had lost nine goals in their opening two matches against Hearts and Motherwell and there wouldn't be any breathing space against Rangers.

'I tried to reason with Dave Halliday. I knew that Harry Yorston had been breaking through while I was away and he had looked a real prospect. Then I pointed out that other, fitter players such as Billy Smith, Dave Shaw or George Samuel could wear the No 4 jersey. Halliday didn't see my side of the argument and bluntly accused me of shirking it. That was the final straw. I was outraged and told him if that's what the board thought of me I wouldn't be playing for Aberdeen at Ibrox. I was prepared and ready to take any consequences. It was a bad day all round as Aberdeen lost 3-1 before a 40,000 crowd.

'The following week I was called into the manager's office at Pittodrie and told that the board had decided to suspend me for four weeks without pay for refusing to play. I accepted their verdict because I'm no shirker. While I was out and finding it difficult to make ends meet without any wages coming in, Aberdeen played further cup qualifying ties against Motherwell, Hearts and Rangers again as well as league games against Partick Thistle and Hibs. And they didn't win one of them. When the ban was served I made an appointment to see chairman William Mitchell and we agreed that things would be no different. My heart was still firmly with Aberdeen and I returned to play against Dundee at Dens Park. I didn't score in that game, but I did hit nine in the following six matches.

'I carry the evidence to this day that I don't and never have shirked a tackle or situation. A couple of years before the suspension blew up we had been playing Irish League side Glenavon in a friendly at Pittodrie. I remember it well, because I finished up with a smashed nose. Jackie Hather played a long ball forward and an Irishman named McLafferty hit me — I thought with his shillelagh. I came out of the clash with a broken nose and looking more like I had gone a few rounds with Rocky.'

Three years after his abortive transfer to Hearts, Gentleman George made another serious blunder when Hamilton went to Hamilton. Again George was ill at ease with his unexpected transfer to Douglas Park. Again it lasted only a few brief months before another return to Pittodrie.

'It didn't take me too long to realise that I had boobed again. Not long after Aberdeen made the breakthrough by winning their first Scottish League title in season 1954-55 the Dons were approached for me by Hamilton Accies manager Jackie Cox. Now Jackie was an old friend of mine and I was persuaded too easily that I would be able to do a job for them. But the truth was that I was a bit slower and on my way out of first-class football.

'The transfer, which involved only a nominal sum, was an eye-opener. No prisoners were being taken in the Second Division at that time and I quickly found out the hard way that if you didn't get rid of the ball rather smartly you came in for the treatment. It wasn't for me and I don't think my body could have stood up to a whole season. But what really convinced me that I had made another stupid move was a League Cup-tie against Rangers.

'Hamilton had done well to hold Rangers in the first leg at home. It was a far different story at Ibrox where we lost six goals and were steamrollered out of the cup. So it was thanks, but no thanks, Hamilton. Until Jackie Cox made his approach I had been playing away happily with the Aberdeen reserves and thinking that football, which had been my life for 18 years, would soon be a thing of the past.

'I had intended all along to make a clean break and to pursue a life outside football when I retired in December 1955. Then a couple of years later Aberdeen offered me a job at Pittodrie as a trainer. I wasn't interested — but I wasn't to get fully out of the game that easily. Dave Shaw had taken over the manager's reins from Dave Halliday and he asked me to look after the reserves on match days. I didn't fancy staying on — and I maybe should have stuck to that train of thought — but I accepted the offer because I believed I could pass on some of my experience to the younger lads.

'It worked for a short while and some promising players progressed. I had taken a leaf out of Dave Halliday's book. He was a great manager and a proper gentleman, and if a

George's grin shows his total delight in Harry Yorston's equaliser in the 1953 Scottish Cup final against Rangers.

player fell short of our requirements or standards I had a quiet word in his ear to remind him of our expectations. That was Halliday's style.

'Then the situation exploded and I finished up by walking out of the Aberdeen dressing-room for the last time in 1959. I had thoroughly enjoyed working with Halliday, but Shaw had a different, more direct approach which went against my grain.

'Aberdeen's second side used to take part in an annual challenge match against a local junior select. The juniors always raised their games to prove they were as good as we were. One game wasn't going too well for us and at half-time Shaw came bursting into the dressing room and started reading the riot act to a couple of players.

'Right there and then I decided that this wasn't for me, so I turned round and walked out. The criticism of the players was too much for me. Dave was under pressure, but I wasn't going to be the one to suffer. His outburst was over the top and I've never changed my mind. He was wrong that night in the dressing-room.

'The break was a clean one now. Dave and I remained friends and some days later I was pleased to receive a letter from the directors thanking me for my services over the years. I appreciated the gesture, although my visits to Pittodrie over the years have been few and far between.'

George still has his own place of affection at Pittodrie. After all, he was part of the side which created a new mould when gleaming silver was brought to the North-East corner for the first time when the Dons defeated Rangers in the final of the Southern League Cup — the forerunner of the League Cup — in May 1946.

'This was the first major final since the end of the Second World War and 135,000 were inside Hampden. It was some game, too, Archie Baird scored with a header in the first minute and I had a header cleared off the line by George Young. Then I slipped a pass to Stan Williams to make it 2-0. Home and dry? Don't you believe it. Rangers came back to make it 2-2 through Duncanson and Willie Thornton. We hit the bar a couple of times before George Taylor shot in the goal to give us the cup. But I don't think there was champagne in the cup — more like lemonade.'

Next year Hamilton and the Dons made it a double, when the name of Aberdeen was inscribed on the Scottish Cup after a memorable 2-1 victory over Hibs. George's emotions were stretched to the limit.

'I thought it was going to be the worst moment of my career when I missed a penalty. We were leading 2-1 as I had scored with a header and Stan Williams had notched an almost unbelievable goal. Then Stan was upended in the box. No doubt about it being a penalty and this was the chance to seal the final. As the Aberdeen penalty-taker I just stepped forward and placed the ball on the spot. Then

It's the medal that means everything to George — the 1947 Scottish Cup victory.

came a wait which seemed to go on for an eternity as Stan received treatment. If he had gone off I would have got on with the job.

'I had a fine penalty success rate, but as I stood there I could feel the nerves getting the better of me. Our homework had been thorough enough and I knew the Hibs keeper Jimmy Kerr was stronger on his left side. When I eventually got round to striking the ball I placed it to Jimmy's left. He brought off a save which left me stunned. I felt dreadful and wished a hole would open up in the Hampden pitch and swallow me. But it all turned out fine for Aberdeen in the end, and no-one was more relieved than George Hamilton.

'The bonus money came in useful. Aberdeen were good at increasing their bonuses for wins. But I have to laugh to myself when I read what some players are earning these days. When I started with Queen of the South I was on £7 a week and this went up to £12 when I signed for the Dons. The wage was increased to £14 — and that's what I was still receiving after 17 years! Bonuses used to operate on £2 for a win and £1 for a draw. But I'm all for players getting as much as they can in their pay packet. It's a good life, but a short one.'

Hamilton couldn't add a second Scottish medal to his collection when the Dons returned to Hampden in 1953 to face Rangers, even after Harry Yorston grabbed a last-gasp equaliser to make it 1-1 and force a replay. Aberdeen couldn't take their second chance and a 1-0 defeat gave Hamilton a runners-up medal. Next season and a similar hard luck story for the Don. A Celtic side featuring greats such as Jock Stein and Bobby Evans, and characters such as Bertie Peacock and Charlie Tully had to be faced. The Dons went down by 2-1 as the Celts celebrated a league and cup double.

Gentleman George won five Scotland caps, including a sensational return to the squad in 1954 when he was all of 36, and turned out twice for the Scottish League.

'It was a pleasant surprise to be asked to join Andy Beattie's World Cup party in Switzerland in 1954, although I didn't play. My sympathy went out to Pittodrie colleague Fred Martin, our first World Cup keeper, when Uruguay fired seven past him. You had to console him. I was proud to have been a member of the Scotland side which beat England 1-0 at Hampden through a Jimmy Delaney goal, but I never truly hit it off in a Scotland jersey.

'There was one exception when we played Belgium and I scored a hat-trick as we won 5-0. But that was an easy game. Then there was a rough-house against Austria in Vienna. A proper débâcle this one. Billy Steel was sent off following an incident and at one point I looked around to see none other than George Young lying flat out on his back after he had come in for some close Austrian attention. This particular Austrian regretted his rash actions. Jimmy Scoular was something of a muscle man

George (centre) celebrates his Scotland call-up in 1954 with Dons colleagues Paddy Buckley and keeper Fred Martin. All three tackled the Norwegians at Hampden . . . and George scored the only goal.

and later in the game he dished out his own brand of football justice.

'For my money, though, the best player of my era was Rangers' Willie Woodburn, a player who knew all about controversy. He was a great centre-half. But, then, Rangers seemed to have them all. George Young was equally effective if not as cultured and Torry Gillick could make the ball talk. But you never knew whether Torry's first love was football or greyhounds. I once looked into the back of his car and it was door to door with straw to make life comfortable for his much-adored dogs.

'Then there was the genius of Billy Steel — even when he was thought to be under the weather. Billy had a reputation for hitting the bright lights and for avoiding the over-vigorous at training. I never saw it affect his play. Just

Gentleman George has taken special care of two prized possessions —
a Scotland cap and jersey.

before we tackled Dundee in one New Year derby one of
our lads announced in the dressing-room that Billy wasn't
looking too good and would give us no trouble. Wrong! He
was devastating and defeated us almost single-handed.

'There were other hard men around the club scene, too.
George Taylor was a smashing half-back and a player you
definitely wanted behind you. If you happened to be target
for rough treatment George would come alongside and
say, 'Don't worry about that bloke. I'll fix him.' He usually
did, too.'

George Hamilton scored 153 goals in 281 appearances
from 1938 to 1955. But that's not all he left the Dons. For

Hamilton was responsible for recommending Archie Glen to manager Halliday. 'I saw Archie play for Annbank United against Kilwinning Rangers and I thought he would make a player. So I told the boss.'

CHAPTER THREE

Archie Glen

If fate and a shrewd piece of judgment on George Hamilton's part brought Aberdeen and Archie Glen together, then destiny surely decreed that the ever-thoughtful midfielder would earn the Dons their first championship flag in 1955.

Penalty kicks, especially when the stakes are sky high, can be testy, nervous and emotional occasions. When the First Division title is the prize, then only stout-hearted men can step forward to place their faith in their boots. Come the hour, come the man. Archie Glen was the man that April 9 afternoon at a Shawfield swollen by a 15,000 gathering.

Aberdeen moved towards Clyde with understandable uncertainty. After all, only five days earlier Clyde had denied the Dons a place in a third successive Scottish Cup final. Out of form, out of sorts — and out of the cup — that was Aberdeen's approach to the Shawfield showdown. If the crown wasn't to be grasped on this trip to the west, then worse appeared to be on the horizon as the next port of call the following week was Parkhead and a Celtic side still nurturing championship hopes.

The Dons had summoned all their grit and determination to survive a semi-final bout with Clyde at Easter Road. Full-back Billy Smith tragically broke a leg before half-time. But the 10 plucky Pittodrie men seemed to be soldiering on towards Hampden again until Clyde made amends for a previous penalty error by snatching a last-gasp equaliser. And it was to be a spot-kick — an accurate effort this time from the previously wayward Robertson — which stopped Aberdeen's three-in-a-row Hampden appearances.

Archie is first to climb the stairs to lead these smart Dons on a relaxing 1954 trip to Switzerland.

So penalties were not far from Glen's thoughts even before referee J. A. S. Bisset made that fateful 13th-minute decision when a Bobby Wishart shot was handled. Without a regular backbone of Smith, Jack Allister and Paddy Buckley, it was to be the sole genuine scoring chance the Dons would encounter that long afternoon.

'Clyde were a very good side at the time and we were aware of what had just happened in the cup. We were also aware of exactly what two more points would mean to Aberdeen.

'Jack Allister and I had been sharing penalty duties. He would take them until he missed. Then I took over. And when I missed the buck went back to Jack. Even though

Jack wasn't on the park that day, it was my turn anyway. Before I hit any penalty kick I always spoke to our keeper Fred Martin and sought his advice on the other keeper's possible reactions. Fred's thoughts were right in line with mine here. Big South African Ken Hewkins was the Clyde keeper and we thought we knew where he was strong and weak.

'So I decided I was going to plant the ball to Ken's left, just above his shoulder line and aimed at the stanchion. I'm pleased to say that's exactly how it worked out. It was the only goal and the points guaranteed the championship for Aberdeen.

'But I had seen ourselves as potential champions at the very start of the season. We were a side getting it together. Instead of wondering what to do or where to look for a team-mate we had this understanding and assurance about our play. When we hit the ball into an area we were confident it would fall to one of our own players.'

Some, like Archie, celebrated quietly on the train journey back north that night. Others let their joy take over. Lanky World Cup keeper Martin, who had kept his goal intact by spreading his long and lean frame to deny Tommy Ring an equaliser, completed the journey on a different level from his victorious mates. He was despatched 'upstairs' to the luggage rack.

'We had taken some beer on board to help with the celebrations and some of the lads went at it as though it was the last day of their lives. I was happy with only a bottle of beer, as I was just so glad and contented we had won the championship. But Fred was blazing and we had to put him up into the rack to keep him out of the way. He's a great character and a very pleasant man. But with Fred out of the way we had more seats for the rest of the lads.

'It was a well-behaved trip back and no-one let themselves or the club down. There weren't too many fans at the station to greet us that Saturday night, but those who were there thanked us for doing the job. It was a job and I was happy to earn a living as a player. When I started out I

Manager Dave Halliday joins Archie and Paddy Buckley on the train journey on the first leg of their trip to Dublin in 1954 for a League international.

couldn't really believe that someone would pay me for playing football.'

Yet if it had not been for a stroll taken by Gentleman George Hamilton one dreary, rainy afternoon the young and slightly-built Glen might have been lost to the senior game. It was a slice of luck which took Lanarkshire lad Archie to junior club Annbank United in the first place.

'I played in schools football when I was just a little over eight. We got some thrashings, too, but I persevered. At that time I didn't think about taking up football professionally.

'Football was my world as a 13-year-old. One afternoon we were due to play at Hurlford, just outside Kilmarnock. When we arrived it was disappointment for me as the pitch was inches deep in water and obviously unplayable. Some of the lads turned around and went home. But if I couldn't play, I wanted to see a game. So four of us made our way to the junior ground.

'These were the days before sports hold-alls and if you carried your boots you tied the laces together and slung them round your neck. It was the only way. We weren't the only ones with long faces, though. As we approached the pitch we could see a man — all anxiety and troubles — marching up and down.

'He asked us if we could play football. Probably he was too worried to take any notice of our dangling boots. He was looking for two players, an outside left and a right half. He was the Annbank manager and he was two short for the kick-off against Hurlford. I had been playing outside left at that time — probably because of my build — so I volunteered to play. That was my introduction to junior football.

'The hacking was a bit much for my 13-year-old legs. But we went on to beat Hurlford by 2-1 and I scored the first goal. After the game I was asked to sign on. First of all, though, my dad, Alex, had to give his permission. He was apprehensive as it was such a big jump going from juvenile to junior at 13. I was the smallest around and the smallest usually played outside left. So outside left with Annbank it was.'

Glen grew in stature and strength and made the move to inside left as his body filled out. Then Hamilton happened by.

'It was only chance which took George to the game. He had been home to Irvine to visit his mother and heard there was a match on nearby. It was a junior cup final and he wanted to see it. By the way, we lost 5-1.'

Manager Dave Halliday has a tight grip on the championship trophy which was secured by Archie's spot-on penalty at Shawfield. A smiling Glen is fourth from the left of the second front row.

The scoreline didn't prevent Hamilton from making an astute recommendation to Dons manager Dave Halliday. Not many players have been pushed along, having been on the end of a five-goal cup final walloping, but Hamilton liked what he saw in young Glen. He appreciated the attitude, commitment and ability. And he told Halliday that it would be worth Aberdeen's time to bring Glen to Pittodrie.

Others, as it happened, had their eyes on Glen, too. For he was also invited to show his talents in trials for Aston Villa and Queen of the South. But in the summer of 1947 Archie — again with permission from his father — became a Don. Halliday, possibly out of frustration and a measure of desperation, turned towards the teenage Glen for a debut on February 19, 1949.

Falkirk, a team lying fifth in the league, had to be tackled by a dispirited Dons at Brockville. Aberdeen hadn't won an away game all season; three months had

elapsed since a victory of any description; and they hadn't
beaten the Bairns since the war. Score — Falkirk 1,
Aberdeen 2. Archie Glen was on his way. His appearances
that term were limited to four games. But he did get off the
scoring mark. That was something of an achievement as
the inside forward didn't get back into the striking charts
until 1954.

Glen's goal arrived in the sleet and rain of a March
afternoon in 1949 when only 750 spectators saw fit to
make their way to Cliftonhill for Aberdeen's visit. Albion
Rovers were a side already doomed to relegation and Glen
had the faithful believing it was all to go wrong again when
he gave the Dons the lead. But Rovers warmed their
meagre gathering with a stunning fightback and a 2-1 win,
their first for five months.

Then a buff-coloured envelope requesting Archie to
swap his red jersey for a khaki Army shirt dropped through
his letterbox. National Service interrupted his Pittodrie
career, but a stint of duty for his country didn't mean the
end of football activities. Far from it.

'I was fortunate enough to captain the British Army
football team. But I think I was made skipper because I was
a second lieutenant and the only officer in the side. We had
a pretty fair team and went on to beat the RAF at Charlton
and the Navy at Molineaux.

'But the Army had a head start on the opposition as we
had that great Welsh giant John Charles playing at centre-
half. What an influence he was. The big man made his
mark wherever he played and none more so than in
Austria, where we took on a select side. We also played in
France and Belgium, but in Austria John let everyone
know what he was about.

'I was playing at right half and John and I always had a
chat about the game just before the kick-off. This time we
noticed the Austrians were fielding a wee, fast centre-
forward. And the Austrian was determined to make a name
for himself by trying to fox John and the rest of the British
side. John believed — and rightly, too, as it turned out —

Archie comes to keeper Tommy Younger's aid in this 1956 1-1 draw with England at Hampden.

that this would-be artful Austrian was the type to try to give his side an early lead. That was the intention, all right, but he picked on the wrong Welshman.

'The Austrian was keen to take on John right away and made a sprint straight for him as soon as he got the ball. That was his big mistake. For he thought he was cunning and skilful enough to slip the ball between John's legs. Charles, too crafty by far, saw it coming and after collecting the ball brushed the Austrian aside with a combination of shoulder and backside. The Austrian was never seen in the game again.'

The Army side also had another bright international star in Manchester United forward Tommy Taylor. Recollections of the Busby babe are tinged with sadness for Glen.

'Tommy played in front of me and he was a special player. He knew his job and there was always an element of surprise about his play. Years later Tommy and I were on opposite sides in a Scotland v England international. It was a pleasure to have known the man and to have played with and against him.

'Tommy died in the Munich air tragedy in 1958. I knew he was in the Manchester United squad, but I didn't know if he had survived. I sat up all night waiting for news to filter through and Tommy was the last person to be named on the casualty list.'

Back on civvy street it was a return to Pittodrie to pursue a professional playing career, even though there were other avenues open. Before the Army's intervention Archie had studied at Aberdeen University during the day and trained with the Dons in the evening. He graduated a BSc in 1950.

But his recall to Dons duty wasn't a happy one in January 1953. Clyde recorded a 3-0 win, not too surprising as the Shawfield side were the league's leading scorers. Having been unable to capture a berth in the 1953 Scottish Cup final against Rangers, Archie switched from his No 10 jersey to the No 6 and a new left-half position. It was here he was truly to make his mark in a half-back line which rolls effortlessly off the tongue — Allister, Young and Glen. Archie was to make it to Hampden for two Scottish Cup finals, but he never left the rostrum with a winner's medal.

'I think we were extremely unlucky in the first one against Celtic. It was terrible in the dressing-room after the game, for there can't be a worse feeling than getting all the way to Hampden and then losing. Alex Young was unfortunate enough to poke a Neil Mochan shot past Fred

Archie turns on the style in this 1959 5-2 win over Partick Thistle at Pittodrie in an unfamiliar change strip.

Martin to give Celtic the lead, but within a minute Paddy Buckley had us level. Then Sean Fallon scored the goal which gave Celtic the cup and league double. And to think we had beaten Celtic in three out of four games that season before Hampden!

'I suppose we had expected to win the cup, especially as we had beaten Rangers 6-0 in the semi-final. It was Jack Allister's turn to take a penalty that day — not mine — and he collected a goal.

'We were back at Hampden in 1959 to face St Mirren. Again, there was to be no happy ending as we lost 3-1. The cup was well on its way to Love Street long before Archie Baird grabbed a consolation in the last minute.'

In between there were highlights, such as the championship breakthrough in 1954/55 and the same Saints had been made to suffer in the 1955 League Cup final. Yet Archie still doesn't have a winner's medal to display, as the Scottish League hadn't issued any.

'Aberdeen were favourites in the final, having gone 13 games undefeated. It was the best record in Britain. But it was still very tight and St Mirren cancelled out an own goal by their Jimmy Mallan. Graham Leggat was the kind of player who could cause confusion to any defence, and that's exactly what he did with just 10 minutes to go. His shot seemed to be harmless enough, but it beat keeper Jim Lornie and gave us the cup.

'Opponents never quite knew what to expect from Graham and that wasn't the only time he caught Lornie out. Graham and I were always looking to do that wee something different at free kicks and we rehearsed various moves at training. All week before this St Mirren game we had been practising a special manoeuvre.

'We got the chance with a free kick about 20 yards out. We discussed the position and decided to have a go. Graham approached the ball and bent forward as though he was about to inspect the lacing. But without straightening up or even looking directly towards goal he hit the ball from his crouched position over the St Mirren wall and into the net. He was that sort of player.'

Archie performed heroically for three Pittodrie managers — Halliday, the man who signed him, Dave Shaw and Tommy Pearson.

'Halliday was a very soft-hearted man in many ways. I

Jack Allister, Alex Young and Archie Glen . . . one of the finest half-back lines ever produced at Pittodrie.

think it was the game we lost 2-1 to Albion Rovers when the pressure really got to him. We were ankle deep in mud and conditions worsened during the match. Halliday was a worried man and at the end he just sat in a corner crying.

'We were also told that we would be having meetings to discuss various points within the club. To my knowledge these never materialised as I believe Dave just didn't have anything to say. He was a collar-and-tie manager and not the best by some way. He could never have been classed as one of the game's great motivators.

'Tommy Pearson was a gentleman, and a very clever left-footed player as well Probably the first time I came across Tommy was when I was studying at university and he was helping out with the coaching. It was a bit of a challenge he issued, too. He stood about three yards from me on the pitch and announced he was going to put the

ball through my legs three times out of three. Naturally, I
didn't think he could. But he did. As a manager I don't
think he was quite as good.'

For all his sterling work for the club — and many
maintain he alone was responsible for saving Aberdeen
from the ignominy of relegation — Archie was only
selected twice for Scotland for the internationals against
Northern Ireland in 1955 and England in 1956. He did,
though, gain seven Scottish League caps and skippered
Scotland's B team against Ireland and England in 1954.

'England scored a goal that never was at Hampden. I had
met up with my former Army team-mate Tommy Taylor
again, but he was in the England camp and one of the
players I was marking. A long ball was played forward and
Tommy and I rose to meet it. The ball was knocked back to
Johnny Haynes and to my surprise he stuck out both arms
to control it and lower it to his feet. As it fell he slammed it
past keeper Tommy Younger.

'I couldn't believe the referee, a Welshman called
Callaghan, would allow the goal to stand. But stand it did.
Graham Leggat scored a legitimate goal that afternoon,
but we had to settle for a draw.'

Season 1959/60 brought the beginning of the end for
Glen through a damaged knee.

'I didn't take much part in the game against Kilmarnock
at Rugby Park, only the opening minutes before I had to go
to hospital with ligament trouble. Bob Wishart played the
ball and Killie centre-half Willie Toner and I went for it.
There was an accidental collision and I knew something
was far wrong with my knee.

'My mum, Elizabeth, was in the crowd that day and she
must have thought she was something of a jinx. When I
had taken my only previous injury — a head knock against
St Mirren — she just happened to be at Love Street as well.

'I did make a comeback from the ligament damage, but
a firm decision was made during the close season. Really,
the specialist didn't need to tell me it was all over. I could

see for myself from his examination when the knee just wobbled about.'

Glen, just like Hamilton before him, had a spell helping the Dons reserves on match day. And, again like Hamilton before him, he called it a day when the air turned too blue.

'Eddie Turnbull had taken over as manager and he told trainer Teddy Scott and me he would be coming down to the rail station to see the reserves off. Eddie didn't believe in putting too fine a point on anything and his language to the reserves left too much to be desired. That was the end of the football road for me.'

Between 1948 and 1960 the tough-tackling player's player made 269 appearances for Aberdeen and scored 27 goals.

CHAPTER FOUR

Graham Leggat

Aberdeen had to look long and hard to find a player remotely capable of fitting into Graham Leggat's familiar No. 7 jersey. For in the years following the international attacker's ridiculously low £16,000 transfer to Luton in August 1958, the Dons tried to fill this major problem position with no fewer than 29 players.

Gifted forwards in their own right, such as George Mulhall, Charlie Cooke, Ernie Winchester, Jimmy Wilson and Jimmy Smith were all handed Leggat's right-wing beat as Aberdeen strained to cope with the loss of this most able and agile player. But circumstances and not Leggat himself dictated the transfer south.

If the Aberdonian caused a stir when he was introduced into the first team in 1953, then he certainly shook up the Pittodrie faithful with his controversial departure to England only five years later. It was never really Leggat's intention to quit an Aberdeen side which had at last tasted sweet success.

'It's never been accurately documented what went on and I've never told my side of the story before. But it really centred around a convenient headline somebody put in the paper — 'I'm Fed Up with Pittodrie, the Press and the Public!' — and the stories which went along with it.

'The person responsible seemed to want all his Ps in the headline so that it looked good. That wasn't the case as far as I was concerned.

'Here's what really happened. I broke my leg twice with Aberdeen and I wasn't long back after the second fracture when I had to report on the Wednesday for my National Service. But the RAF wouldn't accept me, as I believe they didn't want to take the risk.

42

It's more like a wrestling bout as a partly-hidden Leggat tangles with the Celts in the 1954 Scottish Cup final.

'So I never got into the RAF and I was back at Pittodrie in time to play against Queen of the South on Saturday, April 12, 1958. In the paper that night was a whole spread where people had been stopped at random in the street and asked what they thought about me apparently missing out on my National Service. Naturally, many were of the opinion that if their son had to do his bit, then Graham Leggat should go as well.

'There was no way I was standing for every Tom, Dick and Harry in the street telling me what should have been done when I knew the whole truth. I had put up with all the intrusions into my privacy during five years as a professional footballer with Aberdeen and at that point I knew where they could stick it.

'It certainly wasn't my fault I didn't make it into the RAF. In fact, I was desperate to join up. If I'd been accepted I'm sure I would have led a millionaire-style life playing football all over the world for them.'

Leggat, however, had asked away from Pittodrie and in those last few days of April he was quoted in the *Evening Express* as saying, 'Had it not been for the spirit of the team my request would have gone in long before this. For, to be quite frank, I have not been happy at Pittodrie for the last two seasons and I feel that I cannot do justice to the side, or our supporters, in this frame of mind.

'During my lay off, when I was confined to the house, I waited in vain for three weeks for some official of the club to visit me and inquire how my leg was progressing. What do I want? Quite obviously, I want a transfer.'

All these decades later that same Leggat, who had been described as 'an angry young man of soccer', remains adamant he could have re-signed for the Dons had it not been for those off-field events.

'I was very fond of manager Dave Halliday and I think the Aberdeen team was never the same again once he moved to Leicester not long after we had won the championship in 1955. If he had stayed, I would have stayed as well, despite all that had happened in the Press. It wasn't the same without Dave Halliday.

'Halliday was the manager who brought success to Aberdeen with the Scottish Cup and the first championship, but I don't think he ever received the credit or recognition he deserved. There were no stars in the Aberdeen team at that time and that was all down to Halliday, a real gentleman.

'He was a very underestimated manager and his style was to stand back and watch and then make his assessment. His usual soft hat and overcoat were familiar features on the touchline. And Dave was always civil and well-mannered when he spoke to people.

'The spirit and everything else which helped us through those first few years together were destroyed when he left. At Pittodrie we had 11 players who were determined to do their best and the spirit Halliday injected was tremendous. I don't have any doubt that when Dave left for Leicester the team spirit in our dressing-room dropped.

'Dave preferred to stay in the background and that's probably the reason he was so underrated. It was never the same once he was away in England.

'Then we were training alongside Dave Shaw, or Faither as we used to call him, when only a matter of hours later he was made up to manager to replace Halliday. We were supposed to turn right around and start calling him Mr Shaw. That was asking a bit too much, particularly from senior players such as Archie Glen, Jackie Allister and Jimmy Mitchell.

'There's no disrespect intended to Dave Shaw, but I fail to see how you can possibly be Faither and one of the boys one day and then elevated to a Mr Something the next. It just didn't work out and, anyway, I was destroyed when Halliday left.'

The split between Leggat and his home-town team was made in August 1958. But he did leave the fans with a Leggat legacy of glowing memories, with his mixture of skill, grace and deadly finishing, and that winning goal in the 1955 League Cup victory over St Mirren.

'When I look back on the games I played for Scotland, I don't think there are any which spring immediately to mind. But there was one match which did give me immense satisfaction — a 6-0 beating of Rangers in the Scottish Cup semi-final at Hampden on April 10, 1954. Unfortunately, we then lost the final to Celtic.

'This was my first season in the team and that result over Rangers was something extra special. It was a re-run of the 1953 final and it has to be remembered that up until that afternoon Aberdeen had never knocked Rangers out of the competition. And there we were giving them the biggest beating they had ever suffered in the Scottish Cup before a crowd of almost 111,000.

'Joe O'Neil, who had just recovered from a fractured skull, scored a hat-trick. He netted two in the first half — the second with his head — to give us a fine lead at the break before I made it an almost unbelievable 3-0. It was getting on in the game, I think there were only about eight minutes left, when Joe scored his own third.

'Jack Allister was sure with a penalty after Willie Woodburn had fouled Joe, and a late Paddy Buckley header made it 6-0.'

Leggat was a player of breathtaking impact. In his debut season alone he immediately established a post-war record for an Aberdeen winger by notching 19 goals. Football was a natural way of life, but, he says: 'It was never my ambition to be a football player. I used to play with a ball in the morning, noon and night because I enjoyed it. But this was never designed to take me into the professional grades and I think I must have seen Aberdeen play only twice before I lined up for them.

'I had been playing at junior level with Banks o' Dee and things just seemed to flow on from there once I had signed for Aberdeen.

'The Scottish Cup final in 1953 was too soon for me, but I did make my debut on September 12 that year against Stirling Albion. That came after only one game in the reserves, so it could be looked upon as rapid progress. We lost by 1-0, but it was memorable, all right.

'Dave Halliday wanted me to play on the right wing, but that meant having right-half Tony Harris just behind me. Halliday thought that Harris was a bit of a rough guy, and he was right, even though Tony turned out to be my best pal. So he slipped Jackie Allister in behind me for support and moved Tony to the other side of the park.

'Then the half-back line of Allister, Young and Glen developed. And that must rank as one of Aberdeen's best ever — if not the very best. They were a superb blend.

'Really, I had so many good team-mates around me that life was made easy. All I had to do was get the ball over the top of a full-back or around a defence and players such as Jackie Hather or Paddy Buckley would finish it off. I enjoyed scoring, too, but we played as a team.'

The silky Leggat was all too often the victim of crude challenges. Two broken legs, two fractured arms and,

Leggat also made Rangers suffer at Pittodrie. Here he is completing the scoring against George Niven in a 4-0 rout in 1955.

later, a horror knee injury which almost caused his right leg to be amputated would be more than sufficient testimony.

Leggat had confirmed his place as a constant menace to defences and in October 1957 — after scoring for Scotland a few days earlier in a 1-1 draw with Northern Ireland in Belfast — he struck five fabulous goals into the Airdrie net at Broomfield. Graham had been aided that day by the vision and perception of Billy Little, who claimed Aberdeen's sixth and final goal in the last minute.

The combination did, however, inspire one headline writer to come away with the gem of, 'Leggat goals came Little by Little!'

'Not long after I scored those five goals, just about two weeks later, I broke a leg in a league game against Partick

Thistle in a tackle with their full-back Baird. I don't think they wanted me to do the same thing to them!

'But I wouldn't suggest that the injuries I took with Aberdeen were deliberate because these things just happen in football. I took a few injuries in my career, probably more than I should have done, but it was worth it just to get the ball into the net.

'The other break I took with Aberdeen was only a hair-line fracture. So that was nothing too serious, as far as getting back playing was concerned.'

Once those leg breaks had affected his future and taken Leggat not into the RAF but to Craven Cottage, the Scotland winger was to suffer from the cynicism of the Italians, and it left him with an angry weal shaped like an upside down L on his knee.

Fulham had undertaken a close-season tour of Italy. But Leggat's Italian job lasted for only three minutes and led directly to a dramatic chapter in his career. A brutal tackle bared the flesh back to the bone of his right knee and the injury was so cruel that an Italian player who came to help fainted at the sight of the gaping wound.

Frank Osborne, the manager who signed Leggat for Fulham, recalled graphically, 'When I saw him lying there, I thought he would never kick a ball again. The flesh below the knee was flapping loose and there was sand, grass and filth inside the wound.

'He was rushed to Alessandria Hospital, where he became delirious. So serious was his condition that the authorities fixed up a bed for me alongside him. For the next two nights I scarcely slept.

'On the second day the head surgeon told me bluntly he would have to gamble to save amputating Leggat's leg. He wanted to know his medical history and how long it was since he had an anti-tetanus injection.

'I told him I didn't have these particulars with me, but I would cable Aberdeen for the information. 'There's no time for that', was his answer. So the hospital went ahead with what they had to do.

Graham displays the dash which finally dumped St Mirren in the 1955 League Cup final.

'Everything depended on Leggat having good blood. After 24 hours it was obvious he had, for he began to mend.'

The former Don was such a resilient, quick healer he resumed training and was ready for Fulham's opening of the 1959 season, only a month after serious fears had surrounded his future.

Fulham got far more than just their money's worth out of the outstanding Scot. For a start, and a pretty good one at that, Leggat netted in every one of his first six competitive games to equal an English scoring record.

He also showed the superstitious side of his nature by deliberately putting on his left boot before his right. And if Fulham won, Graham kept on wearing the same clothes until they were beaten.

'I remember scoring all these goals in my opening games for Fulham. In fact, I'm sure I scored in my first eight matches. I certainly did have a fine scoring run with 22 goals in my first season, 20 in the next and then 23 the following season.'

Fulham was the centre of nationwide attention when the maximum wage barriers were broken, and Graham did manage to squeeze a canny bit more out of the Craven Cottage kitty with a unique clause in his contract.

'We were on the maximum permitted wage of £20 a week. So, too, was Johnny Haynes, even though he was the captain of England. Johnny made the breakthrough when the wage limit was increased to £100. He got the full £100 — and I received another £5 a week on my basic.

'Johnny made the goals and I scored them, all this despite the gap in our wage packets. I decided at this point I had no chance of getting back into the Scotland team unless I played at outside-right. So I was to be compensated every time Fulham played me out of that position.

'Before re-signing for them I insisted on a clause being inserted in my contract where I would collect an extra £5 every time I was played anywhere except outside-right.

'I was in seven different jerseys for Fulham and this highly unusual bonus helped me make up some of the cash on Johnny. So I was on a basic £25 a week, plus this extraordinary perk.'

If the contract had been in operation the previous season, Graham would have been wealthier to the tune of £150. That would have helped compensate for the loss of any international fees.

Leggat was with Fulham for a little over eight years, scoring 129 goals in 234 league matches. Then at 32 and having been transfer-listed when the club decided to employ the robot-like 4-3-3 tactics of the day — with no place for Leggat's vitality — Graham signed for Birmingham City.

The actual fee was never disclosed, except that

Celtic's legendary Jock Stein (right) keeps a close eye on the situation. But Leggat had the last laugh as he scored the only goal in this 1956 league clash at Pittodrie.

Birmingham paid between £15,000 and £20,000. And that was about the same amount Fulham had handed over to Aberdeen all these years earlier. So Leggat was a sound investment, all right.

He even made his way from Craven Cottage into the Second Division with a touch of class and style. Fulham had been forced to recall the former Don because of their injury situation and Leggat let them know exactly what they had been missing by scoring a hat-trick against Leicester.

During a 16-month association with Birmingham, Graham had an unusual sideline — photographic model! 'This was nothing serious and only gave me some extra pin money. We used to train only in the mornings and I found myself at a loose end in the afternoons. One day I was

Graham's concentration is total as the Dons winger squeezes past Dundee full-back Alex Hamilton. Aberdeen won this 1958 Scottish Cup-tie by 3-1, and Leggat claimed a goal.

asked along to stand in at a photo session and it was only a bit of fun.'

Tommy Docherty was the man who appreciated that Leggat still had a lot to offer and he took him on to two more English clubs, Rotherham and Aston Villa.

'I played alongside Tommy when we were in the international team and against him when we were in the English League. I would never have signed for Rotherham if Tommy hadn't been there.

'Tommy was the only reason I went and I always found him to be very fair and a guy who just loved his football. When I was released by Rotherham, after Tommy had gone, he offered me the job as coach to the youth team with Aston Villa.

'But when Villa fired Tommy early in 1970, I knew it was time for me to go as well. I had pledged my loyalty to one

Graham switches on the power to deliver a telling shot.

man and when he was gone there was no alternative but for me to leave as well.

'I had been there for only six months and Villa were struggling. I had worked with Tommy as the club's head coach and I was used to his ideas and methods. I told them that in fairness I couldn't stay.'

Leggat discovered that Canada was calling and he made the Atlantic crossing in 1971 to become first coach to the Toronto Metros when the club gained a franchise into the NASL. Other posts, such as director of public relations with Carling O'Keefe Brewery and vice-president and managing director of Edmonton Drillers, followed.

The Aberdonian was always in demand for TV interviews and commentaries and fronts a sports programme out of a Toronto studio. 'We don't miss a thing over here. In fact, we probably see more games on TV than viewers back home in Scotland.'

Leggat, the thrustful winger who would be placed in the £1 million-plus category in modern values, won only 18 full Scotland caps. But those who were fortunate enough to savour his play, particularly when he was at his peak, are convinced that number should have been doubled — or more.

CHAPTER FIVE

Bobby Clark

Eddie Turnbull knew a player when he saw one, and Bobby Clark was the Aberdeen manager's first signing at Pittodrie in May 1965. Turnbull, of course, was totally aware of the 19-year-old's vast potential as he had only just left him behind at Hampden with Queen's Park to take over the Dons. Turnbull placed his trust in Clark, calling him 'the best goalkeeper I have ever seen'. His faith was well founded.

The teenage Clark, already well steeped in football through deep family links with Clyde, had turned down the bright lights of London and a £100-a-week payroll with Chelsea to follow Turnbull north. It was a decision that the ever-polite Bobby, who went on to fulfil his early promise in a distinguished career for club and country, would not regret.

Within a matter of days the Turnbull protégé had ousted John 'Tubby' Ogston from the first team — breaking a remarkable run of 180 consecutive first-team games — to make his debut in a Summer Cup-tie against Dundee United. And when Ogston was transferred to Liverpool later that year the heir apparent stepped confidently forward to assume what was to be a rightful position for a decade and a half.

Clark, at one time the record cap holder at Pittodrie, won a full set of domestic honours and fought off stiff challenges for his jersey from more than one serious contender as he served under five different Pittodrie managers — Turnbull, Jimmy Bonthrone, Ally MacLeod, Billy McNeill and Alex Ferguson.

'Players win trophies, but the most important man at any

club is the man at the top. And by that I mean the manager. He's the person responsible for setting the standards, ambitions, training schedules, scouting arrangements and the tactics.

'A real hard man was my first boss. There was a joke we used to often share in the Pittodrie dressing-room about Eddie. Needless to say, it was always told well out of his earshot.

'Eddie had been involved in the Atlantic convoys during the Second World War and it was said he was the only man on the Royal Navy's records known to have attacked a shark! Eddie had a curt manner, but he was a coach long before his time.

'We first came together with Queen's Park, and in pre-Turnbull days training was more like a survival keep-fit course with running up and down the terracing, track work, laps and 100-yard sprints. The order of the day changed immediately with the arrival of our new coach.

'The old methods disappeared quickly into a dim and distant past and players soon found themselves with a ball each and on the playing field. Back in the early 1960s, such things were unheard of. But Eddie had seen for himself with trips to Germany to study their methods. Continental clubs had something new and fresh to offer.

'Suddenly there was talk of 4-2-4 formations, and a young keeper — me — was encouraged to start attacks by throwing the ball to feet rather than go for the traditional punt up the park. Every player benefited from these sessions, which were hard but always enjoyable and interesting.

'Eddie, like the rest of us, had his faults. But it wasn't connected with his football knowledge. It was in his ability to handle people and I don't think Aberdeen saw the best of him until he was complemented by the calm presence of Jimmy Bonthrone.

'Jimmy was the perfect foil for Eddie and I don't know why the pair split. They got on well together, had a mutual respect for each other's knowledge and their diametrically

Right-back Henning Boel watches Bobby parry this shot in a 1970 shut-out against Falkirk. In fact, Bobby went three months without conceding a league goal. A certain Alex Ferguson led the Bairns attack that afternoon and was in constant trouble with referee Bobby Davidson.

opposite personalities blended perfectly. I'm sure the Dons' successes of the 1980s would have arrived a decade earlier if they had stayed together with that side from the early 1970s.

'During the Turnbull/Bonthrone era I learned the lesson that football fame can be a very fragile commodity. We were booed by the fans for just squeezing through a Scottish Cup-tie against Clydebank, and only four ties later those same fans turned out in the streets to give a heroes' welcome to the same team with the cup.

'When Eddie left for Easter Road following that 1970 cup breakthrough, Jimmy was left on his own. Despite his hard work, we all know that nice guys don't win anything.

'Ally MacLeod, always the supreme optimist and extrovert, arrived after Jimmy's departure to lift the club by its mud-filled boots. He convinced everyone with his drive and ambition that good times were just around the corner.

C

'Although his tactics weren't on a par with Eddie's and his training wasn't exactly the ideal school for younger players, he had those magic vibrations. Everyone was stimulated by his bubbly enthusiasm.

'Yet Ally used to annoy me with some of the weird rules he invented during training, particularly at seven-a-side practice games. Goals would be chalked off the score if a player missed badly and sometimes he would add five goals on for a good score. And if there were arguments following his personal calculations, then penalties were awarded.

'In one of these crazy games Ally reckoned our team had lost by 10-8. But I had been keeping an accurate tally and we had actually won by 21-14. But Ally's effervescence was exactly what the club needed at that time.

'There were long, mournful faces at the Beach End when Ally left to take on the Scotland job. Then came Caesar — Billy McNeill — the first Briton to hold aloft the European Cup. Billy came, saw and conquered the hearts of all at Pittodrie. But, just like Caesar, he left before the job was completed.

'Billy, a natural leader, possessed the ability to convince players of their importance to the team. When you went on to the park you felt 10 feet tall.

'In his first full season we came within a whisker of winning the league and cup double. We finished runners-up in the league by a slender two points and the following week we lost the Scottish Cup final by 2-1 to Rangers.

'Billy was a great boss, though, and brought a steeliness to Pittodrie. He also picked up two bargain buys in Steve Archibald and Gordon Strachan, who were signed for a combined fee of around £65,000. When they went their separate ways, Aberdeen must have collected the best part of £1,380,000. Not bad business at all.

'Perhaps it was inevitable Billy would return to his first love, Celtic, and I learned of Alex Ferguson's appointment while I was in Argentina with Scotland.

'He's the manager who has won more trophies than any-

Bobby smothers the ball as the Celts wait to pounce in the second half of the 1970 Scottish Cup final.

one else in the history of the club and his outstanding feats might never be repeated. Yet if there was one criticism of Fergie it was that he didn't fully believe in himself on his arrival at Pittodrie.

'In fact, he seemed somewhat overawed and didn't have the instant impact of McNeill or MacLeod. I worked closely with Alex in developing the club's youth policy and I realised his untapped ability.

'Our Premier League victory in 1980 when we broke the Old Firm monopoly enabled him to blossom until it was just one triumph after another. Alex was full of action. He never stopped moving or thinking, as behind the restless energy was a shrewd brain which worked out all the angles.

'His enthusiasm was infectious, too. The first time we met was in Ayrshire not long after I returned from

Argentina at a Scottish schools under-15 final between Ayrshire and Aberdeen. He introduced himself before kick-off and right away started asking questions about our team, which contained players such as John Hewitt, Neale Cooper and Brian Mitchell.

'Alex has always been a great thinker about the game and later showed that he would go to any lengths to weigh up opponents or any individual. That first meeting displayed his real enthusiasm.'

Bobby, always a firm favourite with the Red Army, has his own hand-picked selection of greats, the Dons who had that special rapport with the fans.

'Top of my list would definitely be Joe Harper, without doubt a real Aberdeen legend. The fans and Joe certainly had something going together. He was their own King Joey and he played for the supporters just as much as he did for his team-mates. Seconds after scoring he would give the fans a royal salute and his subjects always answered the call.

'After scoring a mountain of goals, Joe left for Everton and a Scottish record fee of £180,000. The game following his departure was more of a wake. Knowing it was the end of an era, many fans stayed away and those who went to Pittodrie only inspired Arbroath to an uneventful draw.

'Joe performed adequately for other clubs, but he never recaptured the real *joie de vivre* until Ally MacLeod brought him back to Pittodrie some three years later. His service was again valiant until injury called a halt.

'If Joe was a one-man scoring machine, then that soccer gypsy from Hungary, Zoltan Varga, convinced many he was the most skilful player ever to have graced Pittodrie. Yet his stay was an extremely short one.

'Zoltan was good, and he knew it. He even prompted a team-mate to tell me during a game, 'That guy should be in a bloody circus, not a football team.'

'He expected acclaim from fellow players and supporters, but he never formed a close union with the fans. Zoltan was a master craftsman, confident, assured,

Livewire Lou Macari's close-in header would have beaten most keepers
— but not Bobby.

and he loved showing off. In training he would tease less
gifted colleagues just to show how much in control of the
situation he was.

'Jinky Jimmy Smith was a quiet man without all the
drive and ambition normally associated with professional
players. I doubt if he ever realised that fans were inside the
ground.

'He had a nonchalant style and could despatch passes
with almost careless ease. But he didn't enjoy the
adulation at Pittodrie for too long. Jinky became the
second £100,000 transfer from Scotland when he left for
Newcastle only a matter of weeks after Tommy Craig had
moved on.

'You just had to sit up and take notice of Gordon
Strachan, perhaps the best-balanced midfielder of them
all. Chirpy and cheeky, the fans lapped it up when he was
protesting about an over-zealous tackle or doubting a
referee's decision.

'Gordon appreciated his honoured position with the fans

and always tried hard to fit into a team pattern. Then, again, everyone loves a David v. Goliath confrontation and wee Gordon had just as much success as that other little big man.

'The sight of this wispish player wriggling through opposing defences will long be remembered by the fans. Although he was signed by McNeill, it wasn't until Ferguson arrived that the wee man came into his own.

'Steve Archibald was undoubtedly the biggest financial bargain and his value increased faster than Aberdeen houses during the oil boom years. McNeill brought him north from Clyde for a paltry £25,000 and when Steve signed for Spurs his fee was in excess of £800,000.

'Yet days before Steve came to Pittodrie he almost signed for Ayr United. While Ayr hummed and hawed over the fee Aberdeen stepped in, and I suppose the club's bank manager has been eternally grateful.

'Steve has had his critics, particularly when he played for Scotland. But he was a great player to have in your team. I reckoned that his greatest asset was that he put himself about, occupied defences with his timing and wiry strength and created chances for team-mates.

'Then there was another player, Francis Munro, who must have been the first of the super bargains. Eddie Turnbull wasn't slow to snap him up for only £7500 in 1966 from Dundee United and two years later he was sold to Wolves for £60,000.

'Frannie was a big man and almost every afternoon he had to report back to battle against his weight problems by enduring sweat sessions in the drying room in the days before luxury saunas and the like were available.

'He had a party piece which took some beating. Frannie was an expert at tossing a coin into the air and trapping it on his shoe. Then he would flick it up on to his forehead and finish off the act by allowing the coin to slide into his top jacket pocket. He could play a bit, too.'

Clark trained and played alongside 11 keepers during his total of 17 years as a Don and was responsible for

Bobby getting his point across on the other side of the Atlantic as the Dartmouth College lads benefit from his experience.

fostering the special link that exists between these most isolated of players. But Bobby was such a keen competitor that even when Ernie McGarr eased him out of the keeper's jersey in the late 1960s, he forced his way into the team as a central defender.

'It's often said that keepers are just frustrated centre-forwards, but I didn't get any chances to score when I wore the No 6 jersey at Muirton Park in September 1969. I had been playing outfield in training matches and, naturally, I felt I could do a job for the team there. We lost by 3-1 and Jens Petersen had the shirt back for the following game.

'The team had been going through a sticky spell and I had been playing badly. Eddie Turnbull believed the rest would provide the cure for me, but it was a longer break than most anticipated. For it was just over a year before I regained my keeper's jersey.

'But Ernie and I did write something new into the Scottish football history books. He had been playing so well that we was capped against Eire and Austria, and when I did get back into the Aberdeen side I also played against the Irish at Windsor Park. So Aberdeen became the first club to provide two keepers for Scotland in one season.

'Aberdeen have a fine tradition of supplying international keepers. Back in 1955 Fred Martin was the senior keeper, while Reg Morrison was in the under-23 goal. It was repeated in the '80s when Jim Leighton did his stuff for the big team and Bryan Gunn was a very able under-21 player.

'Now Jim has fairly established himself as Scotland's first-choice World Cup keeper and Bryan features prominently in the senior squad, too. Jim's safe, steady, unshowy and for my money the best example for budding young keepers to follow. His recipe for success is a classic one — lots of ability and an awful lot of hard work.

'Big Ben Gunn is very similar. I once watched him let through nine goals as a 15-year-old. And I still reckoned he had loads of talent. He's already come a long way since moving into the English First Division with Norwich, and he has a long way to go in the game.'

One particular Pittodrie keeper did beat Bobby all ends up. He was the Belgian, signed from Dutch club Twente Enschede, who scored for a Scottish club in a cup-tie on English soil — Marc de Clerk. It was the first and up to now the only goal scored by a Dons keeper in a competitive game.

'Alex Ferguson fixed up my namesake from Holland basically as a cover keeper while I was having problems

Celtic's John Doyle can find no way past Bobby in this no-scoring draw as the Dons marched towards their first Premier title in 1980. Stuart Kennedy is the Don on hand.

with my back and Jim was just breaking through. Marc added some Continental flavour to our routines. And another former Twente player, Theo Snelders, didn't take long to win over Aberdeen fans, either.

'The thing I'm most envious of, though, was that Marc scored in a League Cup-tie at Berwick in August 1980 when his kick-out went sailing into the wee Rangers' net. By my calculations I played a total of 697 games and I don't think I even forced a save!'

Goalkeeping is a serious game, demanding intense and total concentration. But there are lighter moments and there's a friendly side to it, even between fierce club rivals.

'Andy Geoghan, another fine keeper, was a real joker. While we were across in Ireland in 1973 for a UEFA Cup-tie against Finn Harps he secretly got hold of a pass key and swapped all the tall players' suits with the small players' clothing. So next morning there was the sight of long Willie Young appearing for breakfast with a pair of trousers up around his knees. We had a good laugh and then went out and won the game 3-1.

'Goalkeeping, the loneliest position on the park, can prove to be the opposite off it. Keepers can be as thick as thieves when they're together and there was a strong feeling of friendship while I was at Pittodrie.

'By the Sunday afternoon at the end of my first week of full-time training with Aberdeen, most of my digs mates had gone off home and I was beginning to feel a bit lonely. Then Tubby Ogston popped round and we both went out for the evening.

'This was a little gesture, but it set me thinking. Here I was, a young upstart from Glasgow trying to take over his jersey, yet he was considerate enough to take time out to make sure I was settling in. I've always tried to continue the example shown to me by John Ogston.'

Local Aberdeen lad Ogston, of course, moved his talents on to Liverpool. And Clark also had the opportunity to earn his living in England — or at Ibrox with Rangers. Ibrox manager Willie Waddell was aware that Clark could not regain his place from Ernie McGarr, and with 1970 only a few days old he offered midfielder Bobby Watson in exchange.

Clark had appeared as an outfield substitute for Jim Forrest earlier in the season at Ibrox, so Waddell maybe believed he was acquiring two players for the price of one. Waddell, Watson, Turnbull and Clark gathered together in a Perth hideaway hotel and all seemed to be running smoothly. Then Watson, who could not be classed as a Rangers regular, put an end to the two-way deal by revealing he wasn't interested in playing for the Dons.

It was probably just as well for Aberdeen, as the following month Clark was reinstated for a Scottish Cup-tie against Clydebank and on April 11 that year collected his winner's medal.

Stoke City's £100,000 bid for the established Scotland

That's the way to do it, Bobby. The Dons keeper turns another seemingly net-bound shot over the Pittodrie bar.

keeper two years later was a messy on-off affair which split the clubs and left acrimony in the air. Aberdeen had accepted the offer and Clark had travelled to the Potteries and agreed on personal terms. Again, the script went wrong.

Aberdeen insisted that Clark should make his farewell game in a vital league match against Celtic on October 28, 1972, and the signing ceremony was scheduled to take place right after the final whistle. Celtic won by 3-2 and cut-price Stoke tried to take Clark over the Border at a reduced fee.

Stoke director Alex Humphries, a former keeper, had a two-hour meeting with the Dons board before chairman Dick Donald emerged to announce, 'The deal is off and Bobby remains an Aberdeen player. It's a shocking state of affairs.'

The chairman expanded on exactly what had taken place behind those closed Pittodrie doors. 'The signing was to have been a formality. After the match Mr Humphries indicated he couldn't recommend his club to carry through the deal.

'The Stoke director evidently had some knowledge of goalkeeping and he indicated that he was a brilliant judge. He said he would take Clark if we were prepared to reconsider the fee. But it was either a deal or not a deal.'

Bobby had been kept fully informed by the chairman during the late hitch. 'Dick Donald was as honest as could be and told me exactly what was going on. He knew what a move to England meant and asked me if I still wanted to go. But I told him where Stoke could stick their offer.'

New world footballers, from Zimbabwe to New Hampshire, USA, have benefited from Bobby's deep reservoir of experience and teaching ability. And globetrotting Bobby's eyes were opened wide when he had a brush with the unseen powers of voodoo in the heart of deepest Africa.

'I was coaching Bulawayo Highlanders in Zimbabwe and the first hint that voodoo might be involved came when we boarded the bus for an away game. Lying at the back on top of the customary kit of boots and jerseys was a ladder.

'When we arrived at the ground most of the squad

Soaked in bubbly — and lapping up every second. Bobby and manager Alex Ferguson have that look of mutual admiration in the Easter Road dressing-room on championship day 1980.

trooped through the main door and into the dressing-room. But two of the players placed the ladder against the boundary wall and climbed up and over into the ground.

'I watched in disbelief, but no-one questioned their actions. The explanation was that they were afraid a medicine man had placed voodoo spirits at the entrance and they would be put off their game if they came into contact with them.'

Bobby then committed himself to improving and educating the Dartmouth College team in New Hampshire, and his file will be full to overflowing for the 1994 World Cup finals to be staged with all the glitter and razzamatazz only the Americans can switch on.

CHAPTER SIX

Martin Buchan

Martin Buchan holds the unique distinction of being the only player to have captained a Scottish Cup-winning side at Hampden and skippered English FA Cup victors at Wembley. Aberdeen's generally unexpected 3-1 win over a fancied Celtic in 1970 was followed by an equally unpredictable 2-1 triumph for a reshaped Manchester United over Liverpool seven years later. 'Amazing, you spend all these years knocking your pan in and you finish up as a sports quiz question.'

But the thoughtful Aberdonian will go down in the annals of the game as much more than just a casual topic at a supporters' social night.

Buchan, who at 21 was the youngest captain to capture the Scottish Cup, had a bond with the volatile Eddie Turnbull, the often gruff master technician who guided the Dons to that moment of Hampden glory.

'Eddie was simply the best manager I have ever worked with. No-one could rival his knowledge of the game. And, really, that's the only point that matters. The sum total of knowledge of all the managers I have worked with since would not match what Eddie knows about the game.

'He knows the game all the way through the alphabet, right from A to Z. Other managers know their football from Y to Z. He was a hard boss who stood for no nonsense, but there was total respect for his immense knowledge and understanding of football.

'There were differences of opinion, of course, but Eddie was the boss and always won. There was the time we were in Germany for pre-season training and we had these new track suits which made us look like astronauts. Eddie

70

Everyone loves a Union Street parade, especially Martin and the Dons with the Scottish Cup in 1970.

decreed we had to travel to the match from the sports school where we were staying in the track suits and civvy shoes.

'Mutterings of discontent were heard among the lads as they were uhappy at having to wear track suits and ordinary shoes rather than trainers. They felt silly in an assortment of black shoes, brown shoes and blue suede shoes. I told the boss. But he said, "Martin, son, I don't care what the lads think. We are going to the game as instructed."

'I then asked him one question: would he go to a dinner-dance wearing a black tie, dinner suit and a pair of trainers? "No, Martin, but you're all still going to the game as instructed." That was Eddie, he always had the last word.

'Very few managers possess the ability to change a game at half-time, but Eddie was one of them. He could do some great things in that brief spell, whether it was a positional change here, or a word of encouragement there. Managers with this special knack are few and far between, but Eddie had the right words for the dressing-room.

'A couple of weeks before we played Celtic in the 1970 final we had to tackle them in a league game before 33,000 at Parkhead. Celtic were well ahead at the top and odds-on to lift the title. In his pre-match talk Eddie envisaged that the Celts would be sitting in their dressing-room with the champagne on ice and ready to crack the bubbly open to celebrate. Then he delivered a few immortal words and something to the effect — my backside they'll beat us! It worked, as we went out and won 2-1.

'Then in the dressing-room at Hampden on cup final day George Murray, who had scored one of our goals at Parkhead, asked Eddie to deliver the same well selected words. Out they came again and on we went to win the cup.

'Tommy Pearson was the man who signed me for Aberdeen from Banks o' Dee when I was 15, but I had already been training with the Dons for a couple of years. Eddie called me up when I was 17 and I decided to give myself until I was 21 to make it in football. I knew I could still go to university if it didn't work out.

'But with players such as Bobby Clark, Jimmy Smith, Ally Shewan, Jim Whyte and Tommy McMillan, Aberdeen had the makings of a great side. I think the player who impressed me most, though, was great Dane Jens Petersen. He was a thorough professional and I learned a lot from this Aberdeen skipper.

'Then there's Teddy Scott. I went back to Pittodrie with a pal — I always enjoy showing people around Aberdeen and taking them down to the club — and I introduced him to Teddy. I said that this was the man who got me ready for the first team. Teddy replied, "You got yourself ready." I think that sums up the unassuming Teddy. He's had a great influence on the many youngsters who have come through the Aberdeen ranks and there was no-one more

How's this for a prize! Martin, shadowed by Bobby Clark, raises the Scottish Cup.

delighted than I was when he was taken by Scotland to the World Cup finals in Mexico.'

Buchan, however, did suffer from some early teething trouble and self-inflicted wounds.

'I made my debut for the Dons at East End Park in October 1966 and we drew 1-1 with Dunfermline. I was being used more as a marker in those days, but I didn't mind as I was getting a game. By the time November 1968 came around I wasn't featuring too regularly and I felt I should have been in the side. So I wrote out a transfer request.

'Talk about the impetuosity of youth. I was impatient all right, but I don't believe the directors ever saw the transfer request. Before it was presented I was back in the team and the request was withdrawn. All this took place within the space of 24 hours.

'But there was a six-month period from May 1969 when I was out of the team with a broken ankle. I had been at a testimonial match in Inverness and I fell asleep at the wheel while driving home. A pal in the car also broke a bone in his foot.

'The accident happened just outside Alford and the car finished up on its side in a ditch. We were rescued by two lads who were going fishing and they offered to drive us to hospital in Aberdeen. I insisted we should report the accident first.

'They wanted me to wait as they probably feared I'd been drinking. But the strongest beverage I touched at that time was Coke or tomato juice, so there was no problem. I was out for a long time and it was agony standing by and having to watch my team-mates go through pre-season training and early games.'

Jim Forrest had been the Dons skipper, but Turnbull appointed Buchan as club captain in February 1970 , just weeks short of his coming-of-age 21st birthday. He's not likely to forget that first game in charge either.

'We were booed off the pitch at Pittodrie! Fans pay their money, so they're entitled to their opinions and this one certainly wasn't one of our better performances. We had been expected to thrash Clydebank in the Scottish Cup, but we only managed a 2-1 win. In our defence the pitch was very icy and we never warmed up.

'The main thing was that we were through to the quarter-finals and the team was certainly beginning to take shape. That's when Derek 'Cup-tie' McKay, who had been signed on a free transfer from Dundee, emerged as a personality and a player who hit peak form at exactly the right time. Derek had his critics, but he was a great finisher and his goal at Brockville was enough to give us a quarter-final win over Falkirk.

'A transport strike caused havoc with our travel arrangements and we had to go from Stirling to Falkirk in a mini-bus. With Aberdeen players and officials all playing sardines it was one of the most uncomfortable journeys

Captain and manager unite to carry the Scottish Cup out of Hampden.

I've ever experienced. But we were through and into a Cup semi-final against Kilmarnock at Muirton. Cup-tie McKay did it again by scoring the only goal.

'That took us on to the big one. Don't ask me about the final because I don't remember too much about it. You're on a high with the atmosphere generated by a 108,000 crowd and the match seemed to be over in a flash. I only remember the occasion as I have photographs of the game to prove it.

'We had been very calm while preparing at the Gleneagles Hotel, our pre-match headquarters. The match itself remains largely a haze. What I do remember are Joe Harper's penalty, Derek's first goal and being under some serious Celtic pressure. Then lifting the cup high was an extremely proud moment.

'Back at Gleneagles, some of the lads let off steam. I had a couple of beers and went to bed as all I could think about was that we had a game on Monday against Hibs. Yes, we won it too. During the celebrations there were those who thought the team captain was lost. But they hadn't looked around hard enough. I enjoy trying to play the guitar and I was on stage with the band attempting to pick up a few tips from the resident guitarist.

'The reception we received from the fans back in Aberdeen was fantastic. The streets were lined by cheering thousands and that picture stays fondly in my memory.

'The following season was a good one for the club and we finished as runners-up to Celtic in the league. It could have been better, as I believe this is where Eddie may have made his first real mistake.

'Early in the season Joe Harper had been in terrific form and had collected something like 30 goals before the New Year. He was showing everyone he was the best striker in the country. Then in the New Year the goals dried up as Joe went off the boil. I feel that Joe might have benefited from a couple of weeks out of the team. A few games in the reserves and a few more goals would have done the trick. Strikers live on confidence and he would have returned to the team fully refreshed.

'Seven years later and I was at Wembley with Manchester United for another final. Just as Aberdeen had been to Celtic, United were the underdogs to a Liverpool side gunning for a treble. A lot of the Press believed it was a formality for Liverpool, but that was the feeling some of our lads had in the previous final when we played Southampton.

'I was uneasy about that game as too many thought all we had to do was turn up at Wembley and we would be presented with the cup at around 4.45 pm. Every time I watch a video of that Southampton goal, Bobby Stokes seems to get further and further offside.

'It was a memorable defeat. The United fans turned up in huge numbers at the Manchester Town Hall and manager

Tommy Docherty, Scotland manager of the day in 1972, seems to be telling Martin he'll be playing it by the book.

Tommy Docherty spoke for us all when he told them, 'Never mind, we'll go back there and win it next year.' We did just that.

'The Doc was a breezy character and we had a wonderful team spirit at Old Trafford. When we came back into the First Division with the Doc following the trauma of relegation we felt we could give any side a two-goal lead of a start and still beat them.

'There was a perfect blend of youth and experience in the team. Everyone was sharp. It was exciting. Relegation was a blow, but you had to accept you were part of the team. I wasn't happy about being relegated. Far from it. But I was happy to stay at Old Trafford and fight to get us straight back out of the Second Division. We did it in one season, too.'

Following accomplished under-23 international appearances, Buchan had been surrounded by transfer speculation. Manchester United put an end to the rumours by spending £125,000 to take the sweeper to Old Trafford in February 1972.

'It had always been an ambition to play in England. They kept on telling us that theirs was the best league in the world and I wanted to play in the best league. But I never asked for a transfer from Aberdeen.

'Jimmy Bonthrone, who had succeeded Eddie, was very fair and kept me fully informed. He told me that three English sides — Leeds, Liverpool and Manchester United — were interested. It was United who came in with the first concrete bid and I was delighted. United offered me three times the salary I was receiving from Aberdeen. But money wasn't the only reason as I've never been ruled by cash.

'There was something else to look at. Leeds had Norman Hunter playing sweeper and Liverpool had Tommy Smith. So I might not have gone straight into either side and I could only have been used as a squad player. United, on the other hand, were rebuilding and had no-one established in that position.

'When players go in to discuss transfers these days they're usually surrounded by agents, accountants and solicitors. When I motored with Jimmy Bonthrone to Bellshill, it was United who came in with the big guns. For they had Sir Matt Busby waiting.

'During the talks I phoned Eddie Turnbull from the hotel and asked for his advice. If he had said "No" I don't know what I would have done. I also took a look at Aberdeen's league position and decided we wouldn't catch Celtic. If I'd thought we could have overtaken Celtic and gone on to lift the title, then I would have stayed at Pittodrie until the end of the season.

'I now understand that Jock Stein made an inquiry for me just over a year after I moved to Old Trafford and that Celtic were thinking along the lines of cash plus Davie Hay. But I never knew a thing about it and that shows how players can sometimes be the last to know when transfers are on the go.

'Looking at the fee involved back in 1972, Aberdeen must have been happy to let me move. It was a new record for a player being transferred from Scotland to England. Some people thought United had paid out too much money for me. Not long afterwards that record was broken when Everton gave Aberdeen £180,000 for Joe Harper.

'United manager Frank O'Farrell was a nice man. I know there were those who accused him of being aloof, but he couldn't help his manner. I must admit that when I joined United I felt like a country boy journeying to the city. United are a big club in every sense — reputation, tradition, ground and support.

'But I soon realised it wasn't a great team I had joined and the atmosphere was bad. It was as though many players resented O'Farrell and worked against him. Comparisons were made between him and Sir Matt and all was not well.

'The main problem, though, was that United had rested on their laurels since their European Cup win in 1968 and players who should have been replaced were not. Almost inevitably the manager had to carry the can and only a few months after I signed on, O'Farrell signed off. Enter the Doc.

'I'll be perfectly honest and say that some of the players who were still at Old Trafford with O'Farrell weren't good enough to hold down a place with the Aberdeen reserves I left behind. They were bad, but the manager's hands were tied as they were on long-term contracts and he couldn't get rid of them.

'Naturally, there were exceptions and I'm happy to relate that Bobby Charlton was one. Through boyhood, Bobby had always been my favourite player and when you've placed someone on a pedestal there's the danger he'll come crashing down when you finally meet.

'This wasn't the case with Bobby, a gifted footballer, perfect club man and a great professional. George Best's ability also lived up to everything I had expected, even though his career was on the wane. George is probably the most talented player I have seen.

'United were heading for the drop into the Second Division when the Doc stepped into the manager's office. These were trying days, but Tommy relieved the club of the players he didn't want, brought in new faces and rebuilt.

'I enjoyed being a Manchester United player, even though we had some differences. Some folk have seen me as a troublemaker, but I certainly don't share that view. I'll take a stand against the establishment if I think I'm right and I don't see that being interpreted into being a troublemaker.

'United and I came to loggerheads on one occasion when I refused to hand in my passport. They insisted on keeping passports just in case a player reported without his when they were leaving on a European assignment. Out of principle I held on to mine. I pointed out that I was a responsible person and my passport was a valuable and personal document.

'There were other times when I, as captain, was asked to take the players' grievances to the management. But I often found myself standing alone without any back-up and it appeared as though I alone had stirred up trouble.

'The Doc and I had our moments of harmony and disagreement. There was a spell when he played me at full-back. When I made it clear that full-back was no use to me he arranged for Queen's Park Rangers to become my next club for £160,000. The board, I believe, stopped the deal.'

There were, of course, other lighter moments when Buchan displayed his acid wit. 'I think we were playing away at Coventry when this total stranger barred my way from entering the players' lounge. I was always the world's worst at getting out of the bath after a game and the Press were hovering around for quotes. This lad stretched out his arms and asked if I had a quick word for the Press. How about velocity, I replied.'

Buchan was named as Scotland's Player of the Year in 1971, the same year he won his first full international cap. With Scotland he remained his own man, adhering to his principles.

'I suppose I had a stormy international career, but I always wanted to play for Scotland and I was proud to wear my country's jersey. I gained more than 20 caps and it might have been more but for injury and Willie Ormond's general reluctance to change a winning side.

'Most of the time you could hardly fault Willie's selections. They were very sound. He was a completely different character from the Doc or Ally MacLeod and was well liked by the lads.

'But I did feel very bitter about being made a scapegoat when Scotland lost the centenary international to England at Hampden by 5-0. I don't think I had a particularly bad game, but the Glasgow Press were unfair in their criticism after the match.

'I was named by a national newspaper as one of the men who had to go. Bobby Clark was another. I was out in the wilderness until 1974 and West Germany when I was called in after other players pulled out.

'The following year there was another row when I failed to report in Glasgow when the squad assembled. I feel this was a typical example of the SFA making out a timetable and requiring each player to obey their every instruction.

'I had just played three games in five days, yet I was supposed to rush north the following day. Stewart Houston was a United team-mate in the same position. I had been carrying an injury and I felt that I would have been of more use to Scotland if I'd stayed on at Old Trafford for treatment. I would be fit quicker as, quite frankly, Scottish squad facilities at the time were primitive compared with United's.

'The men at the top wouldn't accept the fact that I was a responsible adult and quite capable of acting in the interests of all concerned. These days are gone now.

'Willie Ormond was a nice guy. But he treated me badly at a Wembley incident in 1975 and I wasn't in the habit of apologising to people who did me wrong. Willie shouldn't have said I asked for a second chance after my refusal to go to Rumania for a European Championship tie.

'Here's how it was: Willie told me that I was being saved for the Saturday Home International game at Wembley and I certainly didn't interpret that as meaning I would be sitting on my backside. I phoned my dad, Martin, and he travelled overnight from Aberdeen to see me play against England.

'Three-and-a-half hours before kick-off I was told I would be on the substitutes' bench. I eventually watched the game, which we lost 5-1 by the way, from the stand. Had I known that I wouldn't be in the starting line-up, my dad could have stayed at home and watched the game on TV rather than making a wasted 500-mile dash.

'I told Willie I wouldn't be going to Rumania for our next game. Willie was a good bloke, though, and I'm possibly a lucky man he didn't bear a grudge as I was back as captain of Scotland for the return against Rumania seven months later.'

Tommy Docherty also had the fans howling — some with laughter, others of a different persuasion with rage — when he came out with an infamous outburst after Buchan had been omitted from a Scotland selection. The jersey went to Tom Forsyth and the Doc likened the Ranger to a carthorse while Buchan was a thoroughbred.

'I'm sure the Doc, always controversial, was just being mischievous. I tried to defuse the situation by saying that we both ran for the same stable.'

Then in 1977 Buchan was again accused of temperamental behaviour as far as Scotland and the captaincy were concerned. It's a term he feels is unjustified.

'Ally MacLeod let me down. When he took on the inter-

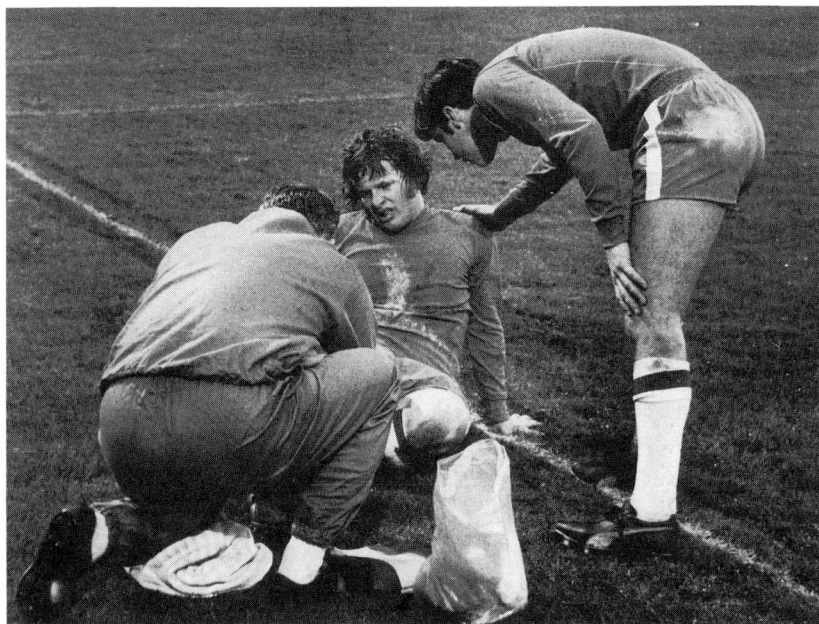

Concerned captain Buchan checks that wee Joe is all right after a hefty Hearts tackle led to a penalty in 1970. King Joey, recovered, rose and rammed in the spot kick for the only goal.

national job he told me he wanted me to be captain for the Home Internationals. Our first group meeting with Ally came right after United had beaten Liverpool in the Cup final. I had played at Wembley with a bad kneee, having injured it in the previous game against West Ham, and how I got through the final I'll never know.

'After our group meeting in North Wales, Ally took me aside and told me of his plans for the captaincy. I said it sounded mighty nice, but I couldn't play because of the knee injury. Ally said not to worry as we were about to go to South America to play Chile, Argentina and Brazil in World Cup warm-ups and I would be captain out there.

'In the meantime, Bruce Rioch was the skipper for the Home Internationals. When we got to Chile, Ally conveniently forgot his promise. Bruce was the captain against Chile.

'A man is entitled to change his mind. But when we first met, Ally told us he would stick by his word. In my view he didn't. Then Bruce was injured and I discovered from the Press that I was to be captain for the next game against Argentina.

'Ally didn't tell me until we were in the dressing-room just before the game. Everybody back home knew I was to be captain. I didn't. Because of the advance publicity I told Ally I would lead the lads out this time. But never again.

'I try not to mess people about and I don't like being messed about myself. I played in the next game against Brazil, but I wasn't captain.

'That was the night we came across a player by the name of Zico. No-one really knew a thing about him until he fired a free-kick into our net. Great Brazilians such as Luis Pereira, Rivelino and Amaral were also playing in that game and I had the pleasure of tackling them again early in 1989 when Brazil hosted the first Veterans World Cup, or the Copa Pele as it was called.

'They were the hosts, made the rules and won the cup. The talent was still there, all right, but the legs couldn't respond so swiftly to the messages being sent out.'

Buchan did cause a bit of a stir back home when he sent a postcard to Jimmy Forbes, former sports writer with the *Evening Express,* from that awful Argentinian World Cup attempt. It read, 'Not missing much.' And it was signed simply 'MB.'

Now at the time there was intense newspaper speculation that Nazi war criminal Martin Bormann was alive and well and living in the depths of Argentina. And his initials just happen to be the same as Buchan's.

Martin diversified his talents from football to guitar plucking to becoming conversant in Spanish. He gained a Higher in the language. 'There were those who believed I was becoming proficient in Spanish because I would be joining Real Madrid. That was a case of adding two and two together and coming up with the wrong number.

'Really, I don't know how I would have reacted or

Young Martin has just been called up by the Dons in 1966 . . . and doesn't he look delighted.

adapted if I'd been given the chance to play abroad. Foreign clubs have gone for British strikers and mid-fielders, players who can create and score goals rather than sweepers who prevent them.

'But I do look back on my career and wonder what would have happened if I'd stayed with Aberdeen; if the team had been kept together; if Eddie Turnbull had remained as manager. Then, again, I could have gone to Leeds or Liverpool. My only regret is that I didn't win a championship medal during my years at Old Trafford.

'My career with United finished in 1983 when Ron Atkinson was manager. I didn't get on with Ron and I felt he got rid of me prematurely. He wanted to shape his own side and players such as Lou Macari and myself, who had been there for a decade, didn't fit in.

'From Old Trafford I had 15 very happy months with Joe Royle's Oldham. But old age — I was 35 — took over and the boots were stored.'

Alex Ferguson and his European Cup-Winners' Cup winners travelled to Manchester to play in Martin's testimonial before he moved on, and the entertaining match finished with honours even at 2-2. It was Ferguson, too, who offered the Aberdonian some sound advice when he tried his hand at management with Burnley.

'Alex phoned me on the Saturday morning of our first game. He told me some golden rules: make yourself available to the Press, because if you don't speak to them they'll write what they want anyway; never seek confrontations; as a manager situations will arise when you have to impose your authority, but don't contrive situations just to show you're the boss.

'I listened intently then went back to the don't seek confrontations bit. Sorry, Alex, but you're a bit late with that one. I just punched so-and-so player three weeks ago.

'After only four months I resigned from the Burnley job. Chairman Frank Teasdale was a very enthusiastic Burnley fan and he offered to go as well. I didn't want him to do that. It was a great experience and one I wouldn't have missed. But if you walk out of a job after only four months, it doesn't give you much credibility with other chairmen.

'Throughout my career I've maintained that football is a simple game made difficult. My philosophy has always been that it takes a good player to pass the easy ball.'

Buchan, a master of the easy ball, made 188 appearances for Aberdeen between 1966 and 1972, scored 11 goals and prevented countless others.

CHAPTER SEVEN

Joe Harper

Joe Harper — or King Joey to give him his more accustomed regal title — was the greatest striker ever to pull on an Aberdeen jersey. The chunky wee man's potent goals power is legendary, yet Scottish football must have served this monarch of Pittodrie a grave injustice.

For Harper was asked only four times by his country to do the job he performed so expertly and consistently at club level. And on two of those all too rare international occasions he was brought on as a substitute.

'The problem was that Rangers and Celtic players were always picked before anyone else. Provincial clubs, or rather players with clubs outwith the Old Firm, were up against it. What annoyed me most, though, was that during my time with Aberdeen I was always Scotland's leading scorer or second top, yet the caps didn't come.'

There was, of course, the infamous Copenhagen Affair when Harper, who was then with Hibs, was banned for life from playing for Scotland along with Billy Bremner, Arthur Graham, Willie Young and Pat McCluskey.

The sentences were later commuted. But the SFA's severe suspensions almost caused Harper to hang up his boots years prematurely.

'I came very close to packing in playing football following the life ban, as we were all judged and sentenced by the SFA without so much as a chance to speak for ourselves. I don't think that said much for those who were running our national sport, and the unfairness displayed left me with a helluva chip on my shoulder.

'Bumper Graham and I were the only two out of the five who ever made a return in a Scotland jersey and I think that proved our innocence.

'I was shattered when we arrived back in Scotland from Denmark to find we had been officially reported to the SFA and later banned from international football. I was so sickened that I was on the point of putting the game behind me and joining my father-in-law's engineering business.

'A Danish journalist who saw the incident wrote an article absolving me. I presented this to the SFA, but they would have none of it and said they had enough evidence to suggest otherwise.

'Here's exactly what happened on that night of September 3, 1975. We were in a nightclub about 15 miles from our hotel in Copenhagen and we were all chuffed at having beaten the Danes by 1-0. I was particularly happy as I had scored the goal.

'I was sitting talking football with this English lad, who was one of the owners of the disco, and an Irishman when an incident happened at the bar where the others were . . . a lamp had been broken!

'When I went over to find out what was going on I was informed that the club staff had already sent for the police, who then demanded the players pay for the lamp. They refused, but I offered to pay for the damage.

'The police turned me down and insisted that those at the bar would have to fork up. Then I offered a compromise — if I could get everyone outside and into a taxi, would they accept that?

'They did, and although there was a bit of a scuffle outside, everyone got away from the scene as quickly as possible. The reason I wanted to make an exit with the others was that I didn't fancy paying for the 15-mile taxi fare myself.

'Arthur was not involved in any of the trouble. He had been a member of the Under-23 squad which had played the previous day in Frederickshaven, and his only 'crime' was that he broke manager Willie Ormond's 1.00 am curfew.

King Joey's perfect penalty has Celtic keeper Evan Williams looking back in frustration in the 1970 classic.

'There was a bit of bother back at the hotel between one of the SFA officials, Jock MacDonald, of Inverness Thistle, and Billy Bremner and Pat McCluskey. When I went into the room Billy and Pat were turning the bed upside down as a prank.

'Jock was angry at first, but he later calmed down and we all retreated to bed. That's what went on and I think the whole situation was blown out of proportion.'

Harper was later to wear Scotland's colours again, even though it's a game the nation would rather erase from the books — that inglorious 1-1 draw with Iran in Ally MacLeod's ill-fated World Cup finals in Argentina. Joe was a late replacement for Kenny Dalglish in what was to be his fourth and final Scotland call.

Copenhagen must have had an influence on this one-man goals machine, as he nearly missed his international debut there in 1972 as well.

'It was an occasion I'll never forget. How could I? For I was locked out of the stadium when I should have been on the pitch!

'I was one of the substitutes and about midway through the second half manager Tommy Docherty signalled for me to get ready to go on. But I felt I had to pay a call somewhere else first before tackling this World Cup qualifier.

'It wasn't too easy to spend a penny, though, as the nearest loo was outside the ground and when I tried to get back in I discovered to my horror that the door was locked. So there I was, standing outside in my Scotland strip sick with worry and banging furiously on a tight-shut door.

'Eventually someone heard my pleas and came to the rescue. I felt as though I had been on the outside for hours and the Doc must have thought I'd gone all the way back to our hotel to use the loo. It didn't stop the substitution and I took over from Jimmy Bone, who had been one of our scorers.

'A neat back-heeler from Lou Macari let me in for a goal. Then I hit the post and Willie Morgan followed up to net the rebound for our fourth goal. But I really didn't expect to be involved.

'The Doc spoke to me at a training session and said I wouldn't be getting a chance this time, but I'd be used in the return. He also told me he had not been particularly impressed with my play. Others had watched me for him and seen how sharp I was and he had noted their recommendations.

'He did add that I would only get a run in Copenhagen if someone was injured. But he kept his word and I was on from the kick-off at Hampden the following month.'

Joe didn't score in Scotland's 2-0 win in his one and only full international at Hampden. And after the Doc departed for Old Trafford, it became obvious that Willie Ormond had different ideas over the composition of the Scotland attack.

While international bosses may have remained strangely sceptical, Aberdeen's Red Army were totally convinced of their burly idol's ability to snap up even a quarter chance. All over the Pittodrie terracing hearts were opened for Harper and he confirmed his everlasting place as their favourite son with that opening goal in the 1970 Scottish Cup final — an ice-cool, precise penalty.

'I knew I had to shut out everything else that was going on around me, such as the reaction of the 108,000 crowd and the jibes coming from certain Celtic players, after Bobby Murdoch had stopped a Derek McKay shot with his arm.

'Their main culprit was Tommy Gemmell, who was booked for throwing the ball away before I could get on with taking the kick. The gamesmanship could have put some players off, but I simply closed my mind to it.

'Billy McNeill was in there, too, stating the Celtic case and I'm sure their in-vain protests stretched for a full eight minutes. They didn't know I really did have butterflies in my stomach.

'I look on that penalty as my best-ever spot kick. I feigned to play it one way and then stuck it to keeper Evan Williams' right. It hit just the right place in the side netting and I'm sure that even if Evan had gone in the direction of the ball he wouldn't have stopped it.

'We all knew that the game was far from over as Celtic would fight every second of the final. At half-time Eddie Turnbull used his special brand of psychology by telling us we should have been a couple of goals ahead.

'What he was really drumming into us was that we could beat Celtic. We had shown we were not concerned or overawed by Celtic's fierce reputation. We knew we could defeat them.

'Celtic staged the customary surge we had anticipated and we were on a knife-edge until Cup-tie McKay did it again with only seven minutes to go. That's when I think I believed the cup was ours. Bobby Lennox did grab one back, but Cup-tie had the last word with our third goal right on time.

'When referee Bobby Davidson blew that final whistle I just wanted to run over and hug every Aberdeen fan inside the old stadium. They were wonderful and it was at that moment I knew the astonishing relationship I had with the supporters was going to mean so much to me during my career.

'It was the greatest day in my life and Eddie Turnbull was certainly the greatest manager I have known.

'Champagne flowed in the dressing-room and poor Jimmy Bonthrone was bundled into the bath — track suit and all. Jimmy was past caring at this high point and didn't mind his soaking.

'Understandable tension had built up during the week and just prior to the game Eddie had been extremely strained. He had possibly shown more signs of nerves than anyone. But, like everyone else in the dressing-room, he was as happy as could be.

'During our pre-match breakfast at Gleneagles the boss had been particularly jumpy. Bobby Clark had ordered an orange juice, but for some reason or other Eddie sprang straight to his feet and refused the drink.

'All the nerves and tension had evaporated in victory and it was a remarkable win as the bookies had written us off at 5-1 long shots while the Celts were 4-11 on favourites to lift the big prize.

'Before we left Gleneagles a wealthy American business-man, who was also staying in the plush hotel, promised he would lay on a slap-up party if we returned with the cup. He didn't flinch when we brought back the silver and his party must have cost him quite a few dollars more.

'The celebrations didn't stop there that weekend, as tens of thousands lined the streets to welcome our open-deck bus back home to Aberdeen. But there was another spontaneous gesture which was thoroughly appreciated by the Aberdeen players and staff.

King Joey turns to salute his loyal subjects at Pittodrie, as Hibs keeper Jim Herriot looks on in vain.

'On our way from Hampden on the Saturday night our coach drew up directly opposite a bus full of dejected Celtic supporters. To our surprise everyone on the bus applauded us. I think they knew what we had achieved.'

King Joe, of course, completed a clean sweep of Scottish medals by featuring prominently in the 1976 League Cup triumph and playing his part in that first Premier title four years later.

There were, however, quite a few scenery changes on both sides of the Border before a knee injury eased him on his way out of the penalty box. But his career almost didn't kick off because of an over-officious doorman.

'I never wanted to be anything other than a professional footballer. I left school in my native Greenock when I was 15 and was delighted when that great showman Hal Stewart asked me to sign for Morton.

'Hal treated me like a son and shortly after I joined the club he told me to turn up at Cappielow for a Summer Cup-tie against Partick Thistle. It was almost 2.30 pm when I arrived at the ground.

'I tried to walk in through the players' entrance, but the doorman, who couldn't distinguish me from a ball boy, ordered me to pay my way in through the juvenile gate.

'I made my protest to the doorman, who thought he was only doing his job, and soon Hal was on the spot to explain who I was. He was pretty annoyed with me for arriving so late — because unknown to me I was in the team.

'So I made my debut on the right wing at the tender age of 15. It was some baptism, too, as we won 1-0 and I scored the only goal against keeper George Niven.'

Just two years later, Second Division Huddersfield paid Morton £45,000 for the teenager who was the highest-scoring winger in Scottish football with 28 goals. Joe deeply regretted the move.

'I didn't like the town and I became homesick. Anyway, there's no way you'll ever find me praising Huddersfield Town FC, because they wouldn't even give me time off to attend my grandfather's funeral.

'They put me into digs quite near the ground, but I was sharing a room with six others. When I saw the standards I knew I had to get out, and after only 18 months in England I asked for a transfer.

'Hal Stewart took me home to Greenock to start me off as a centre-forward. And he did a fair job on the business side, too, as he signed me for a second time for only £25,000.'

Before the season was half way through, a happy Harper had rediscovered his hunger for goals and had 25 on his plate. Naturally, top clubs were interested and in October 1969 an eager Eddie Turnbull paid out a record £40,000 to take the gifted teenager up the road to Pittodrie.

'That was the beginning of three very good years for me. Aberdeen had an impressive set-up and I was working under the best Scottish manager. Eddie was a difficult man to get to know, but he was a man's man, a hard but fair manager and a great coach.

'He could be moody and I worked out a system which told me straight away what kind of day it was going to be. I'd greet him with a "mornin' boss" before training. If the same reply came back, then training and things in general were going to be fine.

'But if Eddie just grunted, then it was definitely a day to stand well back and stay out of his way. Others who weren't so cute suffered if they attempted a joke when the boss was having a bad day.

'I got to know Eddie well and he was a father-figure to me. But he never did any special favours or granted privileges, even though I was his protégé and he was getting the best out of me.

'We had a good atmosphere in the team. It was very workmanlike and there were no stars. I may have been a top scorer, but I was no star, because Eddie wouldn't allow it.'

Harper made his debut for the Dons at Ayr on October 4, 1969, only two days after signing. Dave Robb notched both for Aberdeen in a 2-1 win, as Joe saved his first goal for his opening curtain call at Pittodrie the following Saturday.

Partick Thistle, the side he had beaten on his introduction to the big time four years previously, were to feel Harper's sting again. His late penalty earned the Dons a 2-1 win.

After displaying his expertise in the hard business of steady net-bulging, Everton boss Harry Catterick swooped on Scotland to snatch Harper in an £180,000 overnight pay-out, another record for Pittodrie. Yet Harper's second sojourn in England still wasn't a visit to dreamland.

'It was a whirlwind transfer and came right out of the blue. And it happened on the Friday night before a game at that. At first, Aberdeen weren't going to tell me which club had come in with an offer.

'When they finally revealed it was Everton, I said that was great. I'd heard of Everton, of course, but I had no idea where they came from and I didn't realise it was Liverpool.

'Jimmy Bonthrone picked me up from my Stonehaven home and the next thing I was signing for Everton in the Excelsior Hotel at Glasgow Airport. And I thought I was only travelling for talks.

'I was happy that I'd brought financial security to my family, but I had an empty feeling in my stomach when I realised I was no longer a Don. I think the fans had the transfer confirmed over the tannoy system at Pittodrie, and back in Aberdeen that Satuday night I felt sick when I read the *Green Final's* report on Aberdeen's 0-0 draw with Arbroath.

'On the Monday I was whisked to Goodison Park for a Press conference — and straight into a Scotland v England controversy. A story quoted me as saying Scottish football was inferior to English, but I didn't say that.

'What happened was that I was immediately branded a haggis-basher, even though I had never played in the English First Division. I know it made me highly unpopular in Scotland . . . and there was also a bit of a cold shoulder pushed in my direction in the Goodison dressing-room, too.

'Most of the first-team squad were local Liverpool lads and there was a touch of resentment that a Scot should come in and keep one of their mates out. But I could look after myself both on and off the park — which was just as well — so I got on fine with the lads and there were no real problems.

'In my Goodison debut I helped Everton to a 3-1 win over

World Cup keeper Alan Rough makes the wrong decision as Joe's penalty helps send the Dons into the 1978 Scottish Cup final in a 4-2 semi-final beating of Partick Thistle.

Spurs. Although I missed a penalty — I sent Ray Clemence one way and then put the ball past the post — I rate that 90 minutes as probably the best game of football I have played in my life.

'I made two of the goals for Howard Kendall, as well as hitting the post and the bar to go along with that penalty misjudgment. My name didn't appear on the scoresheet, but the Everton fans in the 45,000 crowd were right behind me and chanted my name as though I was some kind of saviour. I did get off the scoring mark the next week in a 1-1 draw at Chelsea.'

Harper knew all about the intense rivalry between the Old Firm in Scotland, but he was taken aback — or from the back — in his first Liverpool derby at Goodison. But he still left a deep impression on the Anfield Reds.

'I was an early victim of an over-the-ball tackle by Larry Lloyd and when I told him what I thought of his illegal challenge he just whispered in my ear, "Listen, son, you're playing with men down here." I remembered that and a few minutes later I stood back and watched Larry being carried off after one of my elbows accidentally caught him in the face as we went for the ball.

'Another Liverpool player who couldn't keep his nose out of it was Emlyn Hughes. After one skirmish with me Emlyn emerged holding his nose. I think the referee saw the scuffle, but turned a blind eye as there's always a lot going on in these derby matches.

'Before I left Everton, Emlyn and I became very good friends, so there were no grudges. But in the eyes of the Goodison faithful I had become a hero for giving one Liverpool central defender a sore jaw and the other a runny nose, even though we lost.'

But Joe knew his jersey was hanging on a shaky peg when Catterick was shown the door to allow quick-talking Irishman Billy Bingham in. The pair went together like matches and dynamite and the new manager nearly had a player revolt on his hands after he slapped a £100 fine on Joe and two team-mates during a close-season tour of Norway.

'We were out for a meal and arrived back at the hotel about four minutes after the 11 pm curfew had fallen. One of the club's directors had actually been in the restaurant with us and at 10.50 pm he gave us the signal to eat up and get going. We did just that, but failed to beat the clock.

'It was unfair, to say the least. I did lose a bit of form and I think it was down to Bingham's insistence on weight training. He paid out £2,000 for a special machine and after using it four times a week I put on the weight all right — but in the wrong places.

'My sharpness had pared off and early in that second season at Goodison I knew I had to get back to Scotland and preferably with Aberdeen. English football then was powerful and physical and couldn't compare with the skills in Scotland.'

Harper did get his return ticket to Scotland in February 1974 when Eddie Turnbull signed him for a second time — but the £120,000 took Joe not to Pittodrie but to Easter Road and Hibs. Aberdeen, however, had made the first approach.

Joe typically shares his joy with the fans as he proudly shows off his Premier championship medal.

'Billy Bingham called me aside during a training game and told me Jimmy Bonthrone had been inquiring about my availability. I told him I'd jump at the chance of getting back to Pittodrie.

'After Aberdeen made their initial offer, Bingham let it be known in the papers and that's when Hibs came in. The bids seemed to go up by £10,000 at a time, until Turnbull placed £120,000 before the Everton board.

'Bingham put it to me straight and asked me which club I would prefer to go to. Aberdeen were my first choice, but after a brief meeting with his directors he returned to tell me that I would have to sign for Hibs if I wanted back to Scotland.

'Some people thought I went to Hibs because their terms were better, but I had no decision to make. The options were either to move to Easter Road or stay at Goodison.

'I didn't want to continue with Everton, so I met Eddie in Carlisle and signed for Hibs within the hour. The Dons still hadn't given up, because while I was talking to Eddie a call from Aberdeen was placed at my house.

'The caller said I shouldn't sign for Hibs. Aberdeen obviously had something in mind . . . but it was too late.'

Hibs fans never truly took to wee Joe, even when he dished out the goals in his customary fashion.

'Easter Road wasn't the place for me. I was the target of boo-boys who seemed to hold me responsible for the departure of players such as John Brownlie, Alex Cropley, Alan Gordon and Jimmy O'Rourke. But that had nothing to do with me. They wanted me to sign and I did just that.

'Hibs didn't insist on their players staying in the Edinburgh area and I travelled back and forth every day from Glasgow. In fact, there seemed to be East-West cliques and this didn't help foster friendly relations within the club.

'And even when I scored all the goals in a 5-0 romp in a friendly against Nijmegen and in a League Cup final the fans were on my back. I was in a no-win situation.'

Ally MacLeod boldly brought an end to this out-of-sorts episode in Edinburgh when he recruited Harper for the Dons in April 1976 for an almost throw-away fee of £50,000. Harper was back at the North-east home where he belonged and plying his trade before loyal subjects who fairly lapped up his skills.

There was one minor hitch to be overcome before Joe's return was sealed.

'I met Ally in Arbroath a week before the actual transfer went ahead. On that first meeting he impressed me with his exuberance and straightforward approach. I was delighted he wanted me.

'Ally told me that Dave Robb was to go to Hibs as part of the deal. But my heart sank when Dave opted to stay at Pittodrie and I had fears that the move would be off.

'But Ally assured me that there was a place for me at

They all count, no matter the range. And Ayr's Hugh Sproat was caught in a hopeless position with Joe only a couple of yards out. Referee John Gordon made sure it was a legal, onside strike.

Aberdeen whether or not it meant Dave moving to Easter Road. I couldn't play for the first team as Aberdeen were involved in relegation games and I had been fixed up after the deadline.

'I was certainly overwhelmed at the welcome the fans had for me and in my first game — a reserve match at Tynecastle — two busloads of supporters actually travelled to Edinburgh to wish me well.

'Then around 3,000 turned up at Pittodrie and I was chaired from the pitch by the fans after I scored near the end of the game against St Johnstone. The fans continued to pour into Pittodrie for these reserve games and there must have been 5,000 inside the stadium when I scored four of our five goals against Celtic.

Celtic keeper Peter Latchford makes a despairing lunge, but needle-sharp Harper has the ball on its way into the net again.

'But the most enjoyment I got that season was when we went back to Easter Road for another reserve outing. We won by 6-1 and I scored a very satisfying five.

'The loyalty of the fans towards me was the big reason for my desire to return to Pittodrie. When I moved from Aberdeen a lot went out of my football life because I missed those marvellous Dons fans who had given me so much encouragement.

'I consider them to be the very best in Britain.'

In return, Joe would do anything in his power to please his fans, even if it meant beating the pain barrier.

'I was involved in a car crash while we were returning from a wedding reception in Stonehaven. No, I hadn't been drinking, a car just pulled out in front of me. I was taken to hospital and required a total of 48 stitches. I also had three cracked ribs.

'The following week we were playing Hibs and Eddie Turnbull sent me out, stitches and all. I scored two before

Poise and power as Joe is about to hit the Meadowbank net in a League Cup-tie.

half-time and he kept me inside at the break, saying I had done enough.

'Later, there was a game against Rangers and I actually broke my arm in the opening 10 minutes. Doctors gave it a few taps at half-time and put a bandage on it. I completed the game and at full-time it felt really sore.

'We went out for a meal that night, but I couldn't handle a fork and knife and my wife, Fiona, had to cut up my steak. I knew I had to go to hospital and I later emerged with my arm in plaster.

'I had to wear a protective strapping around my arm when I came back against Dunfermline in a Scottish Cup-tie at East End Park. It wasn't much of a hindrance, however, as I scored the only goal.'

In his two marvellous spells with the Dons, Joe Harper — goal scorer supreme — claimed a record 199 goals in 300 appearances.

CHAPTER EIGHT

Willie Miller

Aberdeen fans have been totally convinced for some time — there's only one Willie Miller! And it's doubtful if his granite-like qualities and super successes may ever be repeated at Pittodrie. Miller has been the Red Army's own Captain Marvel, but there are two sides to this most accomplished defender. For there is Miller the man, and there's Miller the myth.

The man — who held aloft all those glittering domestic and European prizes during halcyon days. Indeed, there were seasons when it was distinctly odd to see this great skipper pictured without the Scottish Cup or some other piece of major silverware in his grasp.

The myth — Willie wasn't just a world-class penalty-box defender, but the second referee on the park as well. From dyed-in-the-wool Old Firm fans to the New Firm supporters on Tayside, each one has been convinced at some game or other that Miller should have swapped his familiar red jersey for a referee's black tunic. Complete with whistle, of course.

Yet it's a claim this wonderful club and country servant would strongly refute, even in the face of televised evidence. One of his most controversial eyeball-to-eyeball confrontations with officialdom arrived at Ibrox in 1987 when Kenny Hope was locked in verbal combat with the straight-talking Don in the centre circle.

The capacity crowd and thousands of armchair viewers were waiting for a seemingly under-siege referee to wave the red card after the no-nonsense defender had stoutly argued his case following a typical ball-winning tackle on Kevin Drinkell. Rangers' light blue legion bayed for blood, and not for the first time in Glasgow, either.

104

Willie has that winning feeling again as he hoists the Scottish Cup and another victor's medal in 1983.

The war-of-words clash, inflamed greatly by the crowd, was decidedly controversial. But Miller would debate that the TV pictures did not give a true reflection of the situation. It finished with a booking for Miller and, later, a Scottish Cup ban for the referee. Too lenient, judged the powers-that-be.

Many players are said to have been born old. With Miller it must have been a case of being born old, and a natural moaner. Referees, opponents, team-mates, officials — you name it and Willie had had a girn and a grin in their direction. He's even been known to shout at himself in stern self-criticism if a routine didn't work out to his satisfaction in training.

But there was one instance when Miller honourably held his tongue, kept a firm grip on his emotions and walked away from a nasty and ugly scene. Dundee United's intense manager Jim McLean came perilously close to inciting a riot when he hurredly made his way from the directors' box in the Dens Park stand and sprinted on to the trackside to spit words of hate at Miller during the clubs' 1988 Scottish Cup semi-final marathon.

Tannadice veteran Paul Hegarty had been red-carded in the first half of this tight affair for chopping away at Charlie Nicholas, and McLean believed Miller had used his mouth to influence and rule the referee's decision.

Many players became embroiled in the unsavoury incident. Except Miller. After private half-time talks involving senior police officers it was soon found that the Aberdeen captain had no case to answer. Not so for McLean, who was fined a whopping £4000 by the SFA and banned from encroaching the touchline area for his unruly conduct.

Miller would argue that several of his bookings were a direct result of crowd intervention, yet in his many fruitful years as the Dons leader he has seldom been cautioned for dissent. And the red card count stops at only three. In an area where tough defenders expect to sit out part of the season because of over-robust behaviour, that's a pretty small tally for a key player who was almost an ever-present.

His first solo walk came in the early 1970s when Willie took his frustration out on a player he has since stood shoulder-to-shoulder with on far-flung battlefields in Scotland's cause — Roy Aitken. A not-so-wise Miller swung a boot at the Celt and had the bath all to himself.

Then came a pair of red cards against St Mirren, not the most over-physical of sides at the worst of times. Aberdeen were two-up at Paisley when referee David Murdoch, later to become the Saints publicity officer, sent off mild-mannered Don Ian Scanlon. Then Miller followed on the lonely trek to the dressing-room for a trip on Frank McGarvey, whose flying elbows had just clipped him about the face.

Willie was born in 1955 — the year Aberdeen took the championship for the first time. Here his Pittodrie team-mates help him celebrate his 25th on May 2, 1980. The following day the Dons travelled to Easter Road and secured their first Premier title.

Two innocuous challenges against Saints at Pittodrie during the unproductive Ian Porterfield reign led to an automatic ordering-off. On this occasion Willie didn't even wait to see a flashing red card as he knew only too well what was coming.

But controversy won't overshadow or dim Miller's many astounding achievements. For he skippered Aberdeen to lofty peaks they had only dared dream of — a European Cup-Winners' Cup and a European Super Cup in 1983; three Premier titles in seasons 1979/80, 1983/84 and 1984/85; four Scottish Cups in 1982/83/84 and again in 1986; a League Cup/Skol Cup in 1986.

And for good measure he has also played more Premier matches than anyone else.

There were the doubters and those of different allegiances who whispered secretly that this tenacious defender's career was over and done with when he entered hospital for an overdue cartilage operation in December 1988. The modern-day Dons without the presence of their anchor man was almost unthinkable. But after a couple of minor hitches and a special course at the Lilleshall sports clinic, unsinkable Miller the mighty was back in first-team action three months later, much to the dismay of Premier hit men and terracing speculators who had put a pencil stroke through his name.

'Yet this durable man of substance — once a keeper and even a Highland League striker — didn't believe his future lay in football when he was a wee lad growing up in his native Glasgow.

'A career in football looked a million miles away in my primary school days and I never had much ambition to become a professional footballer until Aberdeen came on the scene. I had seen the inside of a football ground on a couple of occasions when my dad took me to Ibrox and Parkhead. I wasn't too impressed as I preferred to play instead.

'When I did turn out for the Dalmarnock Primary School team I was in goal. They picked the smallest lad and stuck him between the sticks and I had less muscle around my limbs than most of my team-mates.

'But I must have been a fair keeper as I was chosen in a Glasgow Primary School select squad to tour America and I believe we lost only a couple of goals in our four games. Then I put my goalkeeping exploits behind me when I filled out a bit and moved on to John Street Secondary School in Bridgeton.

'I scored a lot of goals — 40 in one season and 60 the next — and was asked along to play for Eastercraigs. It didn't take long before I heard through the grapevine that Aberdeen were showing an interest and their Glasgow scout, Jim Carswell, was running the rule over me.

'Bristol City and Bury took me south for trials, but when Aberdeen moved in I didn't wait to ask too many questions. I didn't have a moment's hesitation in becoming a Don.

It's not often Captain Courageous has been floored. But this time he was flattened by team-mates after clinching the 1985 crown with an equaliser against Celtic.

'Aberdeen's chief scout Bobby Calder had his job down to a fine art. He was the man with all the right words when it came to putting an anxious mum at ease and answering all dad's questions about their son's future in football.

'Bobby came up to the house with a box of chocolates for mum, some cigarettes for dad and a pocketful of sweets for the kids. He needn't have bothered as I had made up my mind that it was Aberdeen for me. Bobby didn't have to persuade me.

'It was a full year later before I eventually saw Pittodrie when I came up during school holidays for a two-week training session. At 16 I put school behind me and took the major step of leaving my Glasgow home for Aberdeen. I was embarking on a career that nearly every schoolboy dreams of. Little did I realise at that time that my dreams were going to come true.'

Eddie Turnbull was the manager who supervised Miller putting pen to paper to become a registered Don in 1971, but one month later that illustrious coach was off to Easter Road to leave Jimmy Bonthrone to get on with the job of grooming the starlet. After a successful striking spell with Peterhead in the Highlands, Miller was recalled and blooded into the first team.

The baptism came on April 28, 1973, at Cappielow when the 18-year-old Miller took over from Arthur Graham as the Dons won 2-1. 'When Aberdeen farmed me out to Peterhead shortly after I arrived at Pittodrie I scored 22 goals. I liked being a striker, but the boss wanted someone with height in the back four of the reserve team and he played me as a double centre-half.

'When my chance came to play in the reserves I went right off form. I think I lacked confidence. In training, few people thought I would ever make a striker. To tell the truth, I almost gave up football. I thought I would be freed at the end of the season.

'I welcomed the chance to play in defence with open arms. I was just so happy to get a game I didn't care where I played. Things just snowballed from there.'

Yes, the teenager on the Pittodrie track is Willie Miller in his pre-moustache days, of course.

Then in August 1973 Miller was handed the No 6 jersey when Henning Boel was injured for the second game of the season, a League Cup-tie against Dundee United at Tannadice. The fairy tale was on its way to becoming a reality.

In the winter of 1975 Ally MacLeod relieved Bobby Clark of the captaincy and handed the on-field responsibility to the 20-year-old Miller. Prophetically, Ally announced, 'I'm looking to Willie Miller to take Aberdeen to the top. A team captain should be more than just the player who calls when the coin is tossed. Willie has all the qualities which a good skipper needs. He shows the other players a fine example on the field.'

Within a year captain Miller had climbed those victory stairs at Hampden to show off the League Cup to the Red Army following that dramatic extra-time triumph over Celtic. And the skipper retraced that familiar path of glory many times during the following years.

In fact, during Alex Ferguson's Midas-like eight years as manager when the free-flowing Dons were sweeping all before them, the Red Army took up position at Hampden not just tingling with anticipation but waiting for Miller to collect another winner's medal as a matter of course.

The ultimate success — victory in Europe — was achieved in Gothenburg's sprawling, rain-soaked Ullevi Stadium on May 11, 1983. That historic occasion is now marked by, among other souvenirs and memories indelibly imprinted on the mind, a series of wooden-framed colour pictures adorning the Pittodrie foyer. The goals, the celebrations, the sheer joy of it all are captured.

Glancing at the photograph of a smiling Miller clutching the European prize in his right hand, his long-standing fellow international defender Alex McLeish commented, 'Ah, we all remember that game well. That was the night Willie won the Cup-Winners' Cup!'

Miller and McLeish developed into an institution and blended together in the way bacon automatically complements eggs. The partnership is, after all, the finest defesive club pairing our Scottish game has ever witnessed, as their enormous haul of caps would testify.

Both are born winners. Both are fiercely determined characters. Even when a striker has managed to squirm from the grasp of one, the other always seems to be waiting in reserve. In fact, Charlie Nicholas, who terminated his English exile with Arsenal to join the international brigade at Pittodrie, had an apt term for Miller — the head waiter.

It was inevitable that Miller's marvellous consistency would attract more than just admiration from other clubs. He found himself a wanted man on both sides of the Border. First of all Sunderland tried to persuade him that life would be more beneficial and rewarding in England. Later, Rangers threw open the Ibrox door, with promises of the captaincy.

Both times Miller decided to stay in his adopted northern city. The Dons had just eased the Old Firm stranglehold on the Premier crown in 1980 when the sleeping giants on Tyneside awakened to discover that Miller was at the end of his contract. But the Geordies had bargained without Miller's deep feelings for Aberdeen, and manager Alex Ferguson, who had prepared to ward off the English advances with his self-pronounced Govan guerilla tactics.

'I looked to the future when I rejected Sunderland's offer to sign me. But to be perfectly frank, I didn't want to go anyway and the fact that Aberdeen granted me a testimonial season, which culminated in a game against Spurs, didn't affect my decision.

'I could have gone to England and filled my pockets with the big cash on offer, and there was a lot of money for me involved in the transfer to Roker Park. But the way ahead appeared to be far brighter at Pittodrie, where we had a glorious chance of winning. I don't think this was matched at Sunderland.

'The Aberdeen system was more suited to me staying in the Scotland team and I didn't want to be involved in a side which might be struggling for its life every week. I didn't want to move anywhere uncertain or unstable.

'Once I'd been shown around the Roker Park set-up and had a man-to-man talk with manager Ken Knighton, it didn't take me long to decide where I would be lacing my boots for the next few seasons. I worried about the set-up at Sunderland.'

Miller was impressed by the Sunderland facilities and the football-daft Geordies he could have been playing in front of. But Ferguson had a more attractive proposition waiting at Pittodrie.

Ferguson was ready to come out of the trenches fighting furiously to retain the services of his World Cup sweeper. He, too, believed a golden road lay ahead at Pittodrie, while the route at Roker was a rocky one. And Ferguson didn't mind telling those who would listen that his championship-winning skipper would be off his head to accept a move.

The street-wise Dons boss laughed off Sunderland's £300,000 approach, adding that he would not accept a penny less than £450,000. Ferguson would probably have knocked back any increased offer as well.

An uncompromising Ferguson said at the time, 'If any club starts talking at a figure below £450,000, it's just ridiculous. The money they've mentioned is what they're paying for reserve full-backs down in England.

'I don't believe Willie will go to Sunderland. He would be off his head to sign for them. Willie's a player who realises that cash isn't everything.

'He has been talking about the new challenge he would face in England. But I've told him to ask himself — would he get success whith Sunderland? I don't think so. We have broken the ice by winning the championship and I'm convinced more success will follow.' So in July that year negotiations came to a close when Willie stayed a Don.

During his formative years in Glasgow, Celtic had noted the name of William Ferguson Miller. But it was arch-rivals Rangers who made positive moves when the star Don — again at the end of his contract — returned from the sun-kissed·World Cup finals in Spain. Rangers must have had a

Having a ball at Pittodrie . . . that's captain Miller.

strong admiration, if not envy, for Aberdeen's considerable achievements with Ferguson and Miller as the Light Blues later tried to persuade the manager to return to his beloved Govan.

'Rangers made a big offer for me,' says Miller, 'but I turned them down more quickly than I had Sunderland. I think it was partly due to the fact that I had enjoyed being part of the Aberdeen team who had destroyed the Old Firm dominance.

'I hadn't dreamed we would finish the season as winners of the European Cup-Winners' Cup and Scottish Cup. But my intuition was right again. I've never regretted my decision to remain with the club.'

Gothenburg and that 2-1 extra-time defeat of the legendary men in white from the Bernabeu Stadium, Real Madrid, will never be surpassed for Miller. But the real performance which stamped his undisputed class all over Europe had not been reserved for an almost underwater Ullevi Stadium. For Miller had greatly enhanced an already considerable reputation in the breathtaking Olympic Stadium in Munich.

Aberdeen had drawn the mighty Bayern Munich in the quarter-finals and those outwith the boundary of the Granite City generally conceded that the German aces would take care of the upstarts from Scotland in their usual efficient and ruthless way.

Bayern, the much-feared kingpins of Europe, oozed with class and bristled with danger. Experieced internationals such as Paul Breitner, Dieter Hoeness and Klaus Augenthaler would stretch the Dons past breaking point, and hit man Karl-Heinz Rummenigge — a threat to any defence on the world stage — was the one-man panzer division to blast Aberdeen out of Europe.

Only trouble was that the script didn't work out that way at all. The Dons limped into the opening leg in Munich without the starting inspiration of Gordon Strachan, and the outcome of their 45th European encounter was said to be a foregone conclusion.

But Miller made the pre-match critics chew their words with the most accomplished and disciplined performance of his club career. Alex Ferguson had given his captain the unenviable role of picking up the rampaging Rummenigge. Then, again, it should have been no surprise as it was Ferguson who named Miller as the best penalty-box defender in Britain.

A thoroughly composed Miller never permitted his concentration to waver or wander for a split second, even when an attempted scissors kick by the marauding German caught the Don straight in the mouth in a tingling incident and knocked out a gold filling.

The tie was interrupted while two of European football's top performers crawled around on their hands and knees searching the Olympic turf for the missing gold piece. It was never found and the wayward Rummenigge boot

Willie and referee Kenny Hope at the height of their verbal warfare at Ibrox.

probably took care of Miller's bonus cash when he visited a dentist on the return home.

Rummenigge and Miller wrapped their arms around each other at the end of the goalless tie as a mark of total respect and mutual admiration. But the £3,000,000-rated Rummenigge knew he had at last come up against a brick-wall defender capable of extracting the sting and fear from his play.

Miller was to repeat the act and deny Rummenigge a European goal through 180 minutes of battle when the sides clashed again at Pittodrie in a pulsating tie which tested the blood pressure of a capacity crowd and left the Germans beaten and bemused. Bayern seemed to have achieved the objective which was beyond them in their homeland when goals from Augenthaler and Pfugler gave them a 2-1 lead with time fast slipping away.

But trickery by Strachan and his partner-in-deception John McMaster allowed McLeish to level with a header.

And before Bayern could regain their composure and re-organise, a supersub was born in John Hewitt, who spun an awkward ball through keeper Muller's legs to book a semi-final berth amid home hysteria and Bayern bewilderment.

The ensuing defeats of Belgians Waterschei and then Real Madrid are part of a proud history. Yet those early winner's medals are still sweet moments for this courageous captain.

'I was first given the responsibility of captaining the team by Ally MacLeod in 1975 and at 20 I was the youngest skipper in the Premier Division. It was a big thrill when we lifted the League Cup in 1976. It was my first success and a cherished moment.

'We had been living under the shadow of the team which won the Scottish Cup six years earlier, but we proved that we were capable of winning trophies. But I didn't think Dave Robb was ever going to get the ball over the Celtic line, as he seemed to take an eternity.

'Then came the championship win when we broke the Old Firm monopoly. There were tears in the eyes of the most seasoned and experienced professionals in our side when the moment of realisation hit us at Easter Road. Cries were circulating all around the ground that Celtic had dropped a point and our five goals against Hibs were enough to give us the title.

'I knew it was all true the second I saw an ecstatic Alex Ferguson dash on to the park for one of the most famous and fastest sprints in the history of Scottish football.

'The manner in which we won the title meant a lot to us. We had to go to Parkhead twice and beat Celtic both times. We did that and we all felt there was no way we were going to lose it after those stunning performances.'

Scotland have also relied heavily on Miller's enormous talent. He made it steadily through the grades from youth to under-23 until that first cap call came in Rumania in 1975. And it was a bit of a shock because the Don had travelled behind the Iron Curtain as a member of the under-23 squad.

Ally oops! Miller tries to make sure his Scotland colleague Ally McCoist of Rangers doesn't win this muscular duel at Pittodrie.

Willie was splashing away in the hotel swimming pool in Bucharest when manager Willie Ormond broke the news of his instant promotion. And having played in a variety of defensive positions when stepping up the ladder, Willie made his senior debut in midfield in the European Championship tie.

In the autumn of 1988 Miller created a new record by gaining his 63rd cap when he led Scotland on to the Hampden turf for the World Cup qualifying tie against Yugoslavia. At that time it made him the most-capped defender in the game and second only to Kenny Dalglish in the SFA's hall of fame.

His commitment and dedication to his country are as total as they have been to his one professional club. Willie kicked off the Andy Roxburgh reign as Scotland's skipper, but injury for the following match in Dublin ruled him out.

Still, Willie tried his best to make it. He shouldn't have been standing on a damaged ankle, let alone contemplating playing with the knock. But he ventured from Aberdeen to the west coast to report as normal and allow the SFA officials and medical staff to assess the extent of the injury for themselves.

It seems a certainty that the skills and knowledge of Miller will not be lost to the game when the sun sets on his playing career. He was even tipped as the man to succeed Alex Ferguson when Manchester United put out their irresistible call in 1986.

'The time wasn't right for me when Alex Feguson left. I thought the pressure of the business commitments I have in town and playing at both club and international level and managing on top of that would certainly have been too much for me to cope with.'

But the last word on this one-off Don must come from Ferguson, the manager he shared so many moments of elation with: 'Willie is quite simply the best defender I have worked with.'

CHAPTER NINE

Gordon Strachan

Wee Gordon departed from Pittodrie in May 1984 with two freshly minted medals tucked safely into his back pocket. For the neat and nifty international inspiration had helped the Dons to a league and cup double before answering all the transfer questions and signing for Manchester United.

And the acclaimed midfielder continued exactly where he left off once he had crossed the Border to Old Trafford by adding an F.A. Cup medal to his tartan collection in his first season as a Red Devil.

'That made it four cup finals in a row I had played in — three at Hampden and one at Wembley — and I was on the winning side in every one. They were all memorable in their own way, but our national ground in Glasgow doesn't have a look-in when compared with that stadium in London. And the F.A. Cup final is regarded as a far bigger occasion, too.

'Wembley is just a better, brighter ground, from the moment you drive up to those twin towers until you walk out in front of the fans. It's the showpiece of the English season, the cup final, and you're not allowed to forget for a minute exactly what that involves.

'Back home, the Scottish Cup final usually means a special half-hour slot on regional TV on the Friday night before the game and newspaper photographs of the lads with cardboard cut-outs of the cup. That's about it.

'No-one seems to go anywhere near over the top about the Hampden final. But in England the whole build-up from the moment you know you're going to Wembley is exciting and stimulating. It was a great feeling taking part in that 1985 final against Everton.

'And I'm not saying that just because we took the cup back to Old Trafford. It had been some build-up and it turned out to be some day with Kevin Moran being sent off and Norman Whiteside getting the winner past Neville Southall in extra time.'

Strachan's £500,000 route to Old Trafford had been saturated in publicity and controversy. His list of admirers throughout Europe included such giants as Hamburg, Bayern Munich, Verona, Fiorentina, Real Madrid, Spurs, Arsenal . . . and, of course, the patient United.

And his farewell game for the Dons led to arguments and disagreements which still raise voices to this day. The flame-haired maestro was, as usual, in the thick of the battle in the 99th Scottish Cup final when Celtic's Roy Aitken, never a shrinking violet, almost separated Mark McGhee's head from the rest of his body.

So experienced Dundee referee Bob Valentine, once he had doused the heat, made Aitken the first player to be sent off in a Scottish Cup final since Rangers' Jock Buchanan in 1929. The partisan Parkhead support, never fans to openly acknowledge the wee man's marvellous ability while in his club colours, held Gordon more than partly responsible.

'I didn't say a thing to Roy. I didn't need to as Doug Rougvie was in there before me and if I were Roy I would rather tangle with me at my size than Doug.

'Big Roy and I get on great and we're the best of mates when we're in any Scotland party. But these things happen in football.

'He stopped one of my team-mates from going past and his actions could have prevented me from getting another medal. I got annoyed, but so would he if the roles had been reversed.

'I did speak to the referee, but that didn't have any influence on his decision to send Roy off. I just said something like, "That tackle was out of order, ref."

'The referee came into the dressing-room before the game and told us plainly that any ridiculous tackles would

If the hat fits . . . and Gordon certainly likes the feel of the Premier championship trophy in 1980.

result in the offender being ordered off. He felt there was an aggressiveness, if not bitterness, in games between Celtic and Aberdeen and he didn't want any of it in a cup final. So he really stuck by his word.'

Victory in 1984 provided Gordon with his hat-trick of Scottish Cup medals when the Dons made it three-in-a-row with that 2-1 extra-time triumph over the depleted Celts. By coincidence, it also brought the curtain down on Aberdeen careers of Mark McGhee and Rougvie.

Mark's mark was to notch the winner before packing his

boots for the Bundesliga and Hamburg. Folk-hero Rougvie shocked a few by signing for Chelsea.

By then, Strachan and his Pittodrie colleagues had been well accustomed to clocking up some overtime in cup finals at Hampden . . . and Gothenburg, of course.

When Alex Ferguson's emerging Aberdeen reached the old stadium for the first time in 1982 in this competition it was the ever-inventive Strachan who finally killed off Rangers' lingering hopes of a fightback. For Gordon grabbed the decisive third in what went down as a 4-1 rout.

'That was a game I thoroughly enjoyed. It was a sunny afternoon and although we took a while to get going we should have finished it off within 90 minutes. But we really turned it on in extra time.

'John McDonald had headed Rangers into an early lead, but Alex McLeish equalised with a curling shot from the edge of the box. It was an exact copy of the goal he scored in training only a day or two before the final.

'Mark gave us the lead when he headed in one of my crosses and then he returned the compliment by laying the ball on after Doug Bell hit the post. I was left looking at this huge goal from only a couple of yards out, but when I came to strike the ball the goal shrunk to the size of a door.

'When the ball went in, I did a spontaneous somersault on the pitch. Later I was told that a fan watching the game on TV at home in Balmedie did exactly the same thing. Only he tumbled into a stone fireplace in his living-room and broke a leg. I paid him a visit the following week.

'Anyway, Neale Cooper made sure that the cup was ours for the first time since 1970 by completing the scoring when he was left with an open goal.

'We had played Rangers the previous Saturday at Pittodrie in our final Premier League game and we scored four that afternoon as well. At that point it was still mathematically possible we could win the championship and we were 4-0 up at half-time through a John Hewitt hat-trick and an own goal from Colin Jackson.

'Rangers tightened up during the second half and, as it

Gordon was only a babe in the arms for Alex McLeish when the Dons made that big breakthrough at Easter Road.

turned out, we didn't win the title. We also needed Celtic to lose at home to St Mirren, but they became champions by winning 3-0.'

Then 12 months later the Dons and their visionary playmaker were back at Hampden only days after their date with destiny in the Cup-Winners' Cup in Gothenburg. Now the Light Blues again stood between Aberdeen and the

Opening day, 1983, and Gordon grabs Aberdeen's first Premier goal of the season against Dundee with a vicious penalty.

record of being the only club outwith the Old Firm to retain the prized silverware this century.

The fresh chapter was written by spring-heeled Eric Black whose deadly header from a McGhee cross, which had spun off defender Craig Paterson, kept the cup in red ribbons. But the generally lacklustre tie brought an eruption of fury from manager Ferguson, despite the fact his side had played with leaden legs and still with the emotions of Gothenburg swirling in their minds.

Strachan later reacted to Ferguson's outburst — and it cost him a £250 fine.

'The boss actually stopped me from opening a bottle of champagne in the dressing-room and at a Press conference he launched into a tirade over our performance. He felt only Willie Miller and Alex McLeish had played well.

Ouch! Gordon in the wars with Rangers Alex Miller as Light Blue Tom Forsyth moves in.

'But we had played our hearts out for the club and we had just won in Europe as well. It has to be remembered that on the last day of the league programme, when we came right back from Gothenburg to beat Hibs by 5-0, we would have been champions if Dundee United lost and Celtic drew. As it happened, they both won as well and United took the title.'

Later that night a headstrong Strachan and his wife, Lesley, walked out of the official celebration function in the Old Course Hotel at St Andrews. Gordon knew his hot-head had led to a blunder and he later apologised to his colleagues. Back at Pittodrie he was called into the manager's office and informed by Ferguson that his early exit had cost him £250.

Strachan, by his own admission, also made a mistake by exclusively telling the *Evening Express* he would be quitting Pittodrie when his contract expired. He gave his reasons.

Ranger Jim Bett, later to move to Pittodrie, prepares to tackle the wee man in the 1982 Scottish Cup final as full-back Sandy Jardine stands at the ready.

'It's not a question of money — it's good at Pittodrie — but a change of scenery is essential to my career. I would be lying if I said I didn't want to see what other countries have to offer.

'I want to leave Scotland because it gets to the stage where playing at places like Firhill and Cappielow twice a season becomes a bit much. I've tasted all the pies there, met all the tea ladies, and I'd like to meet some new challenges.

'I don't see how my game can get any better up here and it could well get worse. Obviously England interests me and I would have no objections about going to Spain or Italy.'

Those words triggered off one of the biggest European manhunts for a Scottish player and it almost became fashionable for a prominent club to declare an interest.

There's not much joy written on Gordon's face as he is hugged by Alex McLeish at the end of the victorious 1984 Scottish Cup final. Understandable, because Gordon knew it was his last game for the Dons.

But it spelt out uncertainty at Pittodrie and now Strachan feels boss Ferguson could have been justified in leaving him out of his trophy-hunting team.

'It was just stupidity on my part and I realise now I should have kept my mouth shut. It wasn't a nice time for me, but I did get on with the job of winning the league and the cup.

'We clinched the title in Edinburgh again, just as we had done in 1980 with that first major breakthrough. Stewart

McKimmie scored his first goal for the club against Hearts and that made us champions for season 1983/84.

'But I knew I was leaving and that made a great difference from the first time at Easter Road four years earlier. It couldn't have worked out better for me tasting my first success at Easter Road.

'I was born in Edinburgh and Hibs were the club I supported since I was a boy of five. On my first visit to Easter Road, Hibs were playing Aberdeen. Charlie Cooke put on a bit of a show and little did I realise I would be playing his role many years on.

'I don't think we were ready for those title celebrations in 1980. We felt it would probably go to the last game when we were due to play Partick Thistle at Firhill.

'But word was passed to the boss that Celtic had dropped a point at Paisley and that gave us our opening success. We felt for senior players such as Bobby Clark and Drew Jarvie more than ourselves. They had been waiting a long time, while we were young and knew there was more to come.

'It was different for me at Tynecastle. Things were happening on the transfer front and I was confused. Between playing and training I was having talks with Alex Ferguson and other teams and it was getting a bit complicated.

'I was thinking over whether I was making the right decision and whether I would be moving to the right place for my wife and family. Then at kick-off time I had to switch off and give the game my immediate and total concentration, or as much as I could summon. It was a hard time.

'If I were a manager in a similar situation I would certainly have a close look at the player in training and carefully assess his performance. I know I would be tempted to leave him out and the boss could have dropped me.'

Strachan, about to slip out of contract, knew he was definitely going. The only question which remained was

Gordon was used to leaving defenders all at sea . . . it probably came from practising on the beach at Aberdeen.

where? The auction eventually seemed to come down to a straight fight between Cologne and Verona.

Indeed, Cologne vice-president Karl-Heinz Thielen was a

spying visitor to Pittodrie, as was Verona manager Osvaldo Bagnoli. However, Old Trafford's ebullient boss Ron Atkinson was planning his own snatch from right under these foreign noses.

But the big-money West German aces and the lira-laden Italians both believed they had privately secured the wanted wee Don.

'I signed an agreement with Cologne, saying that if I did go to West Germany it would be to play for them. But, then, I also signed a similar agreement with Verona. If I decided on Italy I would play for Verona. But these were certainly not hard and fast contracts.'

Gordon had actually been persuaded by a European agent, well known to the Dons management, to put pen to his German agreement in the very hotel Aberdeen were based in at Varzim for their European Cup-Winners' Cup semi-final against Porto.

When Manchester United stepped out of the shadows with their winning £500,000 bid, the German document was placed on the table. But the Italian paper remained known only to a few.

Cologne complained bitterly to UEFA and Gordon's transfer to Old Trafford was held in limbo while the clubs and the UEFA overlords held closed-doors talks in Paris and secret venues in the South of France.

It was decided that the documents were not legally valid, but the outcome was that Aberdeen had to part with cash and Manchester United pledged to play a friendly in Cologne before a much-relieved Strachan moved on.

Ferguson, of course, was later to follow to continue the one-way link between Pittodrie and Old Trafford.

'Believe me, I almost went to Cologne. Their officials were superb and I was really keen to join the club. But the chance of joining Manchester United — the greatest club in the world — proved too much. If I'd decided not to go to Old Trafford I might have regretted it for the rest of my life.

'Big Ron was a good mate as well as being a good

Out of order, Roy! And the red card was to follow for the Celt (extreme right) as he faces up to Gordon in the fiery 1984 final clash.

manager. I thought United would get somebody I knew to replace him and I had this funny feeling that Alex would be coming here anyway.

'Whatever he's got, it certainly works. His tactics and coaching are right and his powers of motivation are effective, too. I was with Alex for many years at Pittodrie and at Old Trafford I learned even more from him.

'He has kept my standard of fitness up because he knows so much about me. I couldn't say how much training I need to keep in shape, but Alex seems to know exactly.

'We had our odd disagreement because it's no problem picking an argument with him. But at the same time I have every respect for the man.'

Strachan, a seasoned World Cup finals campaigner who has teased and tormented the best, is perfectly positioned to spotlight the differences in the brands of football on offer in the Premier League and in England.

Dons fans might not be overwhelmed by his honest conclusions.

'The tackling in England is not as hard as it is in Scotland, not in a true physical sense. But every team in England seems to be on average about three inches taller than those at home.

'I don't think the Aberdeen team I played in would have won the league in England because it wasn't tall enough. I know we had players such as Alex McLeish and Doug Rougvie, who are over 6 ft. But teams down here seem to have seven or so players that size.

'There's a great emphasis on set piece play in England. They work very hard at it and bring all these big guys into play. I'm not saying that because I'm looked on as a wee fellow, as I've been able to handle myself.

'I believe it's also more physically demanding in England. When you go one-up in a game there's every possibility you can still be beaten as teams contain some real scoring talent.

'The top four or five clubs in Scotland are very good. But when you go in front against the Hamiltons or the Motherwells, then that's usually the game finished.'

Super Strachan, who has brought so much joy to so many thousands of fans, is certainly far from finished with the game he went into straight from school in Edinburgh . . . when he rejected a trial period for Manchester United as he had promised to join Dundee.

It was a roundabout road, as he eventually arrived at Old Trafford via Dens Park and Pittodrie.

'Signing for Billy McNeill at Aberdeen in November 1977 meant a big pay rise for me. My wages went up by £15 a week from the £70 I was getting at Dundee. I didn't know what to do with all the extra money! But I knew I was heading towards that first £100 a week pay packet.

'I spent most of my time laughing with Aberdeen, because there was such a great bunch of guys and there was always humour in the dressing-room or when we were together. Really, we grew up together, married together and became fathers at the same time.

'I had been playing steadily for Manchester United and managed to return to the World Cup squad. But early in 1988 I decided it was time to leave, rather than wait to be told I was going from Old Trafford. So I signed for Leeds.

'I want to keep on playing for as long as possible without

making a fool of myself. Then I'm desperate to stay in football because of the camaraderie and because, simply, of the game itself.

'Perhaps I don't want to waken up and join the real world, with rising at 7 am every day and the ritual drive to the office. I love being out in the fresh air and this is the best profession you could ever be in. To get paid for doing something you love is just incredible.'

Often it was just incredible watching the gifted wee man in the 292 games he played for the Dons between 1977 and 1984, scoring 89 goals.

CHAPTER TEN

Jim Leighton

Players are accustomed to undertaking stringent medical examinations and sifting through contracts with a fine tooth comb before attaching themselves to a club. But Jim Leighton must be the only player on record ever to have signed the Official Secrets Act before turning out for a senior side.

'It was a real James Bond affair just because Aberdeen were going behind the Iron Curtain to Yugoslavia. I was working for the Civil Service and although I had been fixed up by the Dons I was still playing for my junior club Dalry Thistle.

'I had turned out on the Wednesday night and I returned home and went straight to bed. Next thing I knew, and during the early hours of Thursday morning, my mum came bursting into the bedroom saying there was an important phone call for me.

'On the other end of the line was manager Ally MacLeod and he asked if I would like to go to Yugoslavia on the Sunday for a game for Aberdeen. I had to make sure that this was no leg-pull . . . and that I wasn't still dreaming.

'But it was the unmistakable Ally, all right, and he explained why he needed me so urgently. Aberdeen were caught in a tight situation without an available keeper.

'Bobby Clark was injured, Ally MacLean had broken a finger in a reserve match and it had just been discovered that John Gardiner didn't have a passport. And I was the only other keeper on their books.

'I was prepared to go into the office and pack in just to take up this chance, but I was offered some time off to go on the tour. Because I was employed by the Civil Service I first of all had to sign the Official Secrets Act when I told them where I was heading.

The championship is back in safe hands at Pittodrie as Jim shows the Premier trophy to the Red Army in 1985.

'I was working in the employment office and for the life of me I don't think the Yugoslavs would have been remotely interested to learn what Joe Bloggs was getting off the dole. But sign the form I had to.

'And I had to make sure I wasn't photographed with any females, just in case they were spies.'

Teenager Leighton then decided to put the Civil Service, the Giro cheques and the Official Secrets Act behind him and take up Pittodrie's full-time offer.

'I had been getting on well in the office for a couple of years and I know I could have stayed in a good job and collected some extra money from playing football part-time. I had played a couple of reserve games for Aberdeen after signing in September 1976 and I enjoyed the taste of it.

'I would never have forgiven myself if I hadn't taken the opportunity. I had to give myself the chance to find out if I was good enough for the professional grades.'

Leighton, now one of the most thrifty of players ever to occupy goal for his country, has answered that question positively since his cloak-and-dagger introduction on the trip into the unknown territory of Kikinda in May 1977. It wasn't the perfect start as a rare Willie Miller own goal made it 2-1 for the Slavs.

'One of the Aberdeen scouts, John McNab, saw me play for Dalry and I was invited to Pittodrie at the same time as Alex McLeish, John McMaster and John Gardiner. There was a tremendous feeling within the club and we were given the first-class treatment. Bobby Calder came with the form for me to sign and I had no hesitation.'

Aberdeen were not the only club to have their sights set on the lean frame of the future international. In fact, Alex Ferguson, who had Leighton as his goal protector during Aberdeen's great glory years and then took him to Old Trafford, was one of the men who wanted the youngster.

'I could have gone to St Mirren, who were being managed by Alex Ferguson, or I could have gone on Morton's books. But St Mirren weren't a full-time club and I was eager to see how I fared with a full-time club in the Premier League. Anyway, Aberdeen were my first choice.

'Ally MacLeod was the manager when Aberdeen expressed their interest. At that stage I remained with Dalry Thistle probably because they were being managed by Eric Sorensen, who was fairly helping me along.

'When Ally left for the Scotland job I was called up by Aberdeen and Billy McNeill farmed me out to Deveronvale in the Highland League. But it was actually Alex Ferguson, who followed on from Billy as the Dons changed bosses in as many years, who gave me my first-team debut.

Jim jumps to punch the ball off the head of the Rangers raider Derek Johnstone as the Dons won this 1985 clash by 5-1.

'Billy explained that I would only be getting a reserve game every three weeks or so as Ally MacLean and John Gardiner were also competing for the place. So he thought I would pick up some valuable experience by playing in the Highland League . . . and I'm glad I accepted his advice.

'I learned a lot from playing regularly for Deveronvale and at a standard higher than I was used to at junior level. I used to train at Pittodrie in the morning, work in a sports shop in the city in the afternoon and pull on the Deveronvale keeper's jersey on a Saturday.

'I was really following in the footsteps of players such as Willie Miller and John McMaster, who benefited from playing in the Highland League. But the four keepers at Pittodrie all assisted each other and we were very close. Bobby Clark is a terrific bloke and he helped me a lot.'

139

Little did Leighton, who was so popular in the Highlands he was named as Deveronvale's player of the year, suspect that an Aberdeen first-team jersey, European involvement and cup-tie football were just around the corner at the dawning of the season in 1978.

Clark was in the familiar No 1 spot when Spurs rolled into Pittodrie for a glamour pipe-opener on August 5. But it turned to tragedy for the international when he badly injured a thumb and only two days later the young Leighton was drafted in to face Middlesbrough. Ferguson stood by the virtually untried and untested keeper for the opening Premier League on the Saturday, a teasing trip to Tynecastle.

'It was some start, as I lost a goal to Eamonn Bannon after only four minutes. That was just about the last thing I wanted to happen in my real senior baptism. But the lads were not put off by the loss of that early goal and we went on to win by 4-1.

'Playing in the Premier League was a different world altogether and I remember reckoning that one first-team outing was worth 30 reserve games in experience.'

Leighton's experience was to take several steps forward that term as he made his European debut in the Cup-Winners' Cup against Marek Dimitrov in Bulgaria and went on to face Fortuna Düsseldorf. And under-21 recognition swiftly came in his direction.

Then 12 months on, injury once more sidelined Clark as the Dons were about to launch their assault on another season. Leighton was by now the obvious replacement, but a wary Ferguson had contacted Middlesbrough about acquiring former international Jim Stewart.

'I knew that if any other keeper came to Pittodrie he would have to prove he was worthy of his place. It only made me work that bit harder.

'Bobby continued to give me great encouragement and coaching and I didn't mean him any harm but I knew the longer he was out of the team the better it would be for me.

Sometimes it hurts to be a keeper. Jim is swathed in bandages after an accidental clash with Hamilton's Willie Jamieson in 1986.

'We had made our way into the final of the Dryborough Cup in 1980 and I told Bobby I had always dreamed of playing for a winning side at Hampden. When I arrived at the stadium there was a telegram waiting for me. It was from Bobby and it read — 'Make your dream come true.'

'We won the cup by 2-1 through goals by Drew Jarvie and Steve Cowan, and winning that trophy gave me a lot of confidence. I felt I could only get better.'

Leighton had to order some silver polish and a special duster to keep the trophies sparkling. In the following years a constant stream of Scottish Cup, League Cup/Skol Cup and Premier medals flowed as the Dons conquered all before them.

And in 1983, with the keeper well on his international

way, came that crowning glory in Gothenburg in the competition which gave Jim his first helping of European football, the Cup-Winners' Cup.

'No-one in our party in Sweden had a semblance of a thought that we were going to lose the final. Such a thing never entered our heads. We weren't over-confident, or anything like that, but we just believed it was our destiny to go out on to the pitch and win it.

'It was only when we were celebrating our 2-1 win over Real Madrid that we wondered what it would have been like if we had lost. We started the game really well and Eric Black might even have scored with a shot which rattled the bar before we got that seventh-minute opener.

'But even when Juanito equalised with that penalty kick only a few minutes later we never lost faith. I'm sure Santillana would have run Alex McLeish's attempted pass-back right out of that soaking Ullevi Stadium if I hadn't brought him down!

'Real had really done nothing to seriously threaten us, but they were back in the game with that penalty. And I suppose the half-time whistle came at the right time for us.

'West German Uli Stielike looked capable, but we put Neil Simpson on him and his power diminshed during the second half and extra time. Alex Ferguson had approached the final calmly and this rubbed off on the players. He was still cool and methodical as he spoke to us in the dressing-room at half-time.

'Many teams could have crumbled at the thought alone of tackling one of the most famous clubs of the lot. And having a lead pegged back could have rocked a few, too. We never let it interfere with our concentration or preparations.

'The manager had tried to exert some influence on Real by keeping them waiting for the pitch at our final training session the day before the game. But after beating a club such as Bayern Munich in the quarter-finals, we knew we were capable of bringing the cup home.

'I think Aberdeen were out of this world in that period of

Gorebridge referee Jim Duncan flashes a yellow card at an annoyed Leighton following a flare-up at Ibrox. Peter Weir turns away in disgust.

extra time. But there was a very late scare for the marvellous 12,000 fans who made their way by boat and plane to Gothenburg to see history being made.

'Salguero, who had replaced a tired Stielike, rifled a twice-taken 20-yard free kick only a centimetre past my left-hand post in the dying seconds. There were those in the ground who believed the ball had flown right through the net.

'While the Spaniard was lining up to take the kick everyone around could hear Peter Weir call for Divine intervention. 'Please God, don't let him score,' he cried out as he helped form a defensive wall. I think it was just out of nervous excitement.

'But Peter needn't have worried, as I had the shot covered!

'It was a result which cheered not only the Aberdeen fans

and the Scottish public, but the whole nation, I'm sure. And I think you'll go a long way before you see a better game.

'I put on a video of the game almost every second week and it still gives me a lump in my throat. I never tire of watching this achievement and I'm sure I'll still be proud to show it to my grandchildren.

'A lot of people might have fully expected us to win the cup had we got through to play a team such as Waterschei, whom we beat in the semi-final, in the final itself. But the fact that we went out and beat Real Madrid will stay in memories for ever.

'We couldn't have been any wetter when we eventually trooped off the park, but we stayed in the showers, all singing, for fully half-an-hour. Maybe we didn't want the moment to end.

'And our reception back in Aberdeen was both staggering and emotional. It was one of the longest journeys I have ever undertaken . . . and it was a complete pleasure. I've been told there must have been a welcome committee of 100,000 because there wasn't a gap in the crowd from the airport to the city centre to Pittodrie.

'I'm sure the fans could almost touch the harmony and spirit we had in the team. Winning certainly helped, but we had an added ingredient.

'Only a couple of days later we went on to beat Rangers in the Scottish Cup final in extra time through an Eric Black goal. Alex Ferguson wasn't too pleased with our performance and he let everyone know. But he later apologised.

'Then we confirmed our European standing by beating Hamburg in the Super Cup. We didn't so much beat them, but destroy them, and after leaving West Germany with a no-scoring draw they knew they were lucky to get away from Pittodrie with only a 2-0 defeat.

'We had played Hamburg before, of course, in the UEFA Cup. We lost to them, just as we had done to Liverpool in the European Cup.

Jim flies through the air with the greatest of ease to keep out Dundee United's Billy Kirkwood.

'But we learned from these games. We remembered what we had been taught and I don't think we would have won the Cup-Winners' Cup, but for the lessons of Hamburg and Liverpool.

'When we played at Anfield in 1980 the boss sent on two 16-year-olds for experience when the tie was obviously beyond us. They were Neale Cooper and John Hewitt . . . and it was Hewitt who headed in the winner in Gothenburg.'

Leighton was a quick-learning keeper when Jock Stein included him in the Scotland squad for the 1982 World Cup finals in Spain. In October that year Jim took over the jersey from Alan Rough and started with a typical shut-out against East Germany at Hampden. Now he has savoured the unique atmosphere of tackling World Cup finals and is on his way to becoming Scotland's most-capped keeper.

His reflex actions, energy and immense concentration

have simply enhanced his considerable reputation over the years in the international arena. Only three players — Leighton and his former Pittodrie colleagues Willie Miller and Alex McLeish — appeared in all eight qualifying games for the 1986 finals in Mexico. And it was Leighton who really confirmed Scotland's place once more among the elite with a breathtaking display in the play-off in Australia.

'I think the qualifying tie I played against Iceland in Reykjavik was probably the best game I've ever had for Scotland. And to think it was a match I certainly looked like missing through a late injury.

'It's difficult to decide which was your best save, or most important one, or even best game. There's always another match.

'But if I hadn't stopped that penalty in Iceland when the score stood at 0-0, I don't think Scotland would have gone to Mexico. If we had lost that goal we would have needed to go to Cardiff and beat Wales to qualify once more . . . and we just didn't do that.

'It took a goal in the closing minutes from Jim Bett, who played in seven qualifying matches, to give us the win we wanted over Iceland. We had flown there on the Saturday night in high spirits after Richard Gough had headed in the only goal against England at Hampden. But we always knew Iceland were going to be very hard to beat.

'There was quite a drama going on out of the public view, too. I had injured myself in training on the Monday. I was in spasm and the pain was searing from my neck right through my whole body.

'The lads went to the pictures in Reykjavik on Monday night, but I was sprawled out in bed. And flat out it was, too, as I could hardly lift my head from the pillow.

'On Tuesday morning I could barely get out of bed and I sat on the team bus at training, well out of the way. I honestly didn't see any way I was going to be fit enough to play.

'Alex Ferguson, who was Jock Stein's assistant with the

Simply spectacular! Team-mate Brian Irvine and Celtic striker Andy Walker look on in admiration of this acrobatic leap.

international squad, tried to lighten matters by sitting down beside me and saying he had once played with a broken back and scored a hat-trick.

'Then I was given some muscle relaxants and to my

great surprise I found that the prescription eased the ache enough for me to play. I was lucky to turn out, as there was only one side I could turn to without a pain still shooting through my body.

'So when the penalty came I knew in advance that I was going down to my left. When their player struck the ball I dived in the only direction I could and managed to stop the ball going over our line right at the post.'

The injury was a recurring secret complaint between Jim and the Dons and it took two full years before he was eventually given the all-clear from a specialist. If Iceland brought cool Jim's finest hour, then those glittering finals produced his most memorable international appearance.

'That arrived in Queretaro in our section game against West Germany. We had opened against Denmark, and lost by 1-0, but I didn't have to handle the ball too much in that one.

'The Germans beat us by 2-1, but it's an occasion that will stay with me for ever. Gordon Strachan scored our only Mexican goal and the stadium was the best, the atmosphere was tingling and we were up against one of the most formidable and disciplined sides to be found anywhere.

'After the game their keeper, Harald Schumachar, came up to me and said, 'I think Scotland are a very unlucky side.' In our final game against Uruguay I had to make what was termed a spectacular save from Cabrera. But I only got the ball because he hit it close to me.

'Against West Germany Klaus Allofs put in a header and I had to get right across the goal to stop that one going in. So that had to be my best save in Mexico. It must have been agony for the rest of the team playing in the heat at that altitude. I went chasing after a ball when it was hit wide and it took me 15 minutes to recover.

'However, personal glory means nothing if the side fail to achieve their goal. I was pleased to get some saves in, but I would much rather we qualified for the second stage for the first time and I had been totally anonymous.

'I would happily have been called the world's worst if it meant Scotland getting through.'

Leighton, a player with a perfect attitude, will never have such a defamatory statement placed alongside his name. And, after all, he is responsible for making a few English pundits choke on their bad-taste jokes about the alleged ineptitude of Scottish keepers. Leighton has long since pulled the curtain down on this music-hall humour.

'So much rubbish has been spouted by panels and individuals that you can't take it seriously. They can say what they like, but it never affected me either way.'

Even though Scotland didn't win a game in the land of tortillas and tequila, participating in those chilli-hot finals did influence the class keeper. For all these miles away from home he began to feel the need to stretch his legs and walk away from Pittodrie.

Leighton, of course, was still a player under contract at Aberdeen and he was fully prepared to honour that agreement for its remaining two years before joining forces with Alex Ferguson at Old Trafford for a reported £750,000 in May 1988.

Although Leighton never announced publicly that he would be leaving the Dons until the last game of his contract had been played, it was surely the most open secret in Scottish football. Manchester United were always the front-runners and favourites, although Spurs and equally wealthy West German and French clubs also had their representatives sounding out the situation.

'I devoted 13 years of my life to Aberdeen, so when the time came to move on I found it very hard indeed. I had many friends and could recall umpteen great times with the club, the players and the supporters.

'On the Saturday night of our last game of the season I attended a supporters' club dance at Dyce. I had made the decision to go, but I was choked up when I started talking to the lads about Gothenburg and all our other successes.

'Big decisions can never be easy to take, but I had actually made my mind up two years previously when I came back from Mexico. I needed a new challenge because after the highs of Mexico the following two years were a slog and a lean time for me personally.

'I found it hard to motivate myself, even under Alex Ferguson, and before Ian Porterfield took over. My mind was made up, but I actually informed the club I would not be signing on again when we lost to Dundee United in the Scottish Cup that year.

'At one point I was linked with more clubs than I knew there were in Europe! So it was a weight off my shoulders when I was eventually able to turn round and tell everyone I was going to Manchester United.

'I had always hoped to play for them. Ian Porterfield called to say Aberdeen had accepted United's offer and shortly afterwards Alex Ferguson phoned. Within about 10 seconds arrangements were made for me to fly to Manchester.

'Genuine interest had been expressed by foreign clubs and the money on offer was unbelievable. I know I could have made lots more cash in going to the continent, but the minute Manchester United came in, money was forgotten.'

Leighton may have surrendered nine goals in his opening six internationals, but he soon established himself as Scotland's shut-out king, a title which was his deserved possession at Pittodrie.

FULL INTERNATIONAL CAPS WITH ABERDEEN

GEORGE HAMILTON — 5

1946 — v   Northern Ireland
1951 — v   Belgium, Austria
1954 — v   Norway twice

ARCHIE GLEN — 2

1955 — v   Northern Ireland
1956 — v   England

MARTIN BUCHAN — 2

1971 — v   Portugal (sub), Belgium

BOBBY CLARK — 17

1967 — v   Wales
1968 — v   Holland
1970 — v   Northern Ireland
1971 — v   Portugal, Wales, Northern Ireland, England,
            Denmark, USSR, Belgium
1972 — v   Northern Ireland, Wales, England,
            Czechoslovakia, Brazil, Denmark
1973 — v   England

JOE HARPER — 3

1972 — v   Denmark (twice, one as a sub)
1978 — v   Iran (sub)

GRAHAM LEGGAT — 7

1956 — v   England, Wales
1957 — v   Northern Ireland
1958 — v   Hungary, Poland, Yugoslavia, Paraguay

GORDON STRACHAN — 28

1980 — v   Northern Ireland, Wales, England, Poland,
            Hungary (sub), Sweden, Portugal
1981 — v   Northern Ireland, Portugal
1982 — v   Spain, Holland (sub), New Zealand, Brazil, USSR,
            East Germany, Switzerland, Belgium

1983 — v   Switzerland, Northern Ireland (twice, once as a sub), Wales, England, Canada (three times, once as a sub), East Germany

1984 — v   England, France

JIM LEIGHTON — 35

1982 — v   East Germany, Switzerland, Belgium

1983 — v   Switzerland, Wales, England, Canada (twice), Uruguay, Belgium, Northern Ireland

1984 — v   Wales, England, France, Yugoslavia, Iceland, Spain

1985 — v   Spain, Wales (twice), England, Iceland, East Germany, Australia (twice)

1986 — v   Israel, Denmark, West Germany, Uruguay, Bulgaria, Republic of Ireland, Luxembourg

1987 — v   Republic of Ireland, Belgium, England

WILLIE MILLER — 63

1975 — v   Rumania

1978 — v   Bulgaria

1979 — v   Belgium

1980 — v   Wales, England, Poland, Hungary, Sweden, Portugal

1981 — v   Israel (sub), Northern Ireland (three times), Wales, England, Portugal

1982 — v   Holland, Brazil, USSR, East Germany, Switzerland

1983 — v   Switzerland, Wales, England, Canada (three times), Uruguay, Belgium, East Germany

1984 — v   Wales, England, France, Yugoslavia, Iceland, Spain

1985 — v   Spain, Wales (twice), England, Iceland, East Germany, Australia (twice)

1986 — v   Israel, Rumania, England, Holland, Denmark, West Germany, Uruguay, Bulgaria

1987 — v   England, Brazil, Hungary, Luxembourg

1988 — v   Saudi Arabia, Malta, Spain, Columbia, England, Norway, Yugoslavia

ABERDEEN FACTS

HOW THE CUPS WERE WON

European Super Cup
Season 1983-84

First leg — Hamburg 0, Aberdeen 0.
Leighton; Cooper, Rougvie, Simpson, McLeish, Miller, Strachan, Hewitt, McGhee, Bell, Weir.
Second leg — Aberdeen 2 (Simpson, McGhee), Hamburg 0.
Leighton; McKimmie, McMaster, Simpson, McLeish, Miller, Strachan, Hewitt (Black), McGhee, Bell, Weir.
Aggregate — Aberdeen 2, Hamburg 0.

European Cup-Winners' Cup
Season 1982-83

Preliminary round — first leg — Aberdeen 7 (Black, Strachan, Hewitt, Simpson, McGhee, Kennedy, own goal), Sion 0.
Leighton; Kennedy, McMaster, Simpson, McLeish, Miller, Strachan, Black (Weir), McGhee, Bell (Rougvie), Hewitt.
Second leg — Sion 1, Aberdeen 4 (Hewitt, Miller, McGhee 2).
Leighton; Kennedy, McMaster, Simpson, Cooper, Miller, Strachan (Black), Bell (McLeish), McGhee, Hewitt, Weir.
Aggregate — Aberdeen 11, Sion 1.

First round — first leg — Aberdeen 1 (Hewitt), Dynamo Tirana 0.
Leighton; Kennedy (Black), McMaster, Bell (Cooper), Rougvie, Miller, Strachan, Simpson, McGhee, Hewitt, Weir.
Second leg — Dynamo Tirana 0, Aberdeen 0.
Leighton; Kennedy, Rougvie, Cooper (McMaster), McLeish, Miller, Strachan, Simpson, McGhee (Hewitt), Bell, Weir.
Aggregate — Aberdeen 1, Dinamo Tirana 0.

Second round — first leg — Aberdeen 2 (McGhee, Weir), Lech Poznan 0.
Leighton; Cooper, McMaster, Bell (Kennedy), McLeish, Miller, Strachan, Simpson, McGhee, Black (Hewitt), Weir.

153

Second leg — Lech Poznan 0, Aberdeen 1 (Bell).
Leighton; Kennedy, Rougvie, McMaster (Cooper), McLeish, Miller, Strachan, Simpson (Watson), McGhee (Hewitt), Bell, Weir.

Aggregate — Aberdeen 3, Lech Poznan 0.

Quarter final — first leg — Bayern Munich 0, Aberdeen 0.
Leighton; Kennedy, Rougvie, Cooper, McLeish, Miller, Black (Strachan), Simpson, McGhee (Hewitt), Bell, Weir.

Second round — Aberdeen 3 (Simpson, McLeish, Hewitt), Bayern Munich 2.
Leighton; Kennedy (McMaster), Rougvie, Cooper, McLeish, Miller, Strachan, Simpson (Hewitt), McGhee, Black, Weir.

Aggregate — Aberdeen 3, Bayern Munich 2.

Semi-final — first leg — Aberdeen 5 (Black, Simpson, McGhee 2, Weir), Waterschei 1.
Leighton; Kennedy, Rougvie, Bell (Cooper), McLeish, Miller, Strachan, Simpson, McGhee, Black (Hewitt), Weir.

Second leg — Waterschei 1, Aberdeen 0.
Leighton; Kennedy, Rougvie, McMaster, McLeish, Miller, Hewitt, Simpson (Angus), McGhee (Falconer), Watson, Weir.

Aggregate — Aberdeen 5, Waterschei 1.

Final — Aberdeen 2 (Black, Hewitt), Real Madrid 1. After extra time.
Leighton; Rougvie, McMaster, Cooper, McLeish, Miller, Strachan, Simpson, McGhee, Black (Hewitt), Weir.

Scottish Cup
1947

First round — Aberdeen 2 (McCall, Cooper), Partick Thistle 1.
Johnstone; Cooper, McKenna, McLaughlin, Dunlop, Taylor, Botha, Hamilton, Harris, McCall, Williams.

Second round — Aberdeen 8 (Hamilton 3, Harris 3, Williams, Botha), Ayr United 0.
Johnstone; Cooper, McKenna, McLaughlin, Dunlop, Taylor, Botha, Hamilton, Williams, Harris, McCall.

Third round — Aberdeen 1 (Millar), Morton 1.
Johnstone; Cooper, McKenna, McLaughlin, Dunlop, Taylor, Millar, Hamilton, Williams, Harris, McCall.

Replay — Morton 1, Aberdeen 2 (McCall, Hamilton).
Johnstone; Cooper, McKenna, McLaughlin, Dunlop, Waddell, Millar, Hamilton, Williams, Harris, McCall.

Quarter-final — Dundee 1, Aberdeen 2 (Williams 2). After extra time.
Johnstone; Cooper, McKenna, McLaughlin, Dunlop, Taylor, Harris, Hamilton, Williams, Baird, McCall.

Semi-final — Arbroath 0, Aberdeen 2 (Williams 2).
Johnstone; Cooper, McKenna, McLaughlin, Dunlop, Taylor, Harris, Hamilton, Williams, Baird, McCall.

Final — Aberdeen 2 (Hamilton, Williams), Hibs 1.
Johnstone; McKenna, Taylor, McLaughlin, Dunlop, Waddell, Harris, Hamilton, Williams, Baird, McCall.

1970

First round — Aberdeen 4 (Harper 2, Robb 2), Clyde 0.
McGarr; Boel, Kirkland, Petersen, McMillan, Buchan, Hamilton, Robb, Forrest, Murray, Harper.

Second round — Aberdeen 2 (Forrest, Robb), Clydebank 1. .
Clark; Boel, Kirkland, Murray, McMillan, Buchan, Willoughby, Robb, Forrest, Hamilton, Harper.

Quarter-final — Falkirk 0, Aberdeen 1 (McKay).
Clark; Boel, Murray, Petersen, McMillan, Buchan, McKay, Hermiston, Forrest, Hamilton, Harper.

Semi-final — Kilmarnock 0, Aberdeen 1 (McKay).
Clark; Boel, Murray, Hermiston (G. Buchan), McMillan, Buchan, McKay, Robb, Forrest, Hamilton, Harper.

Final — Celtic 1, Aberdeen 3 (Harper, McKay 2).
Clark; Boel, Murray, Hermiston, McMillan, Buchan, McKay, Robb, Forrest, Harper, Graham.

1982

Third round — Motherwell 0, Aberdeen 1 (Hewitt).
Leighton; Kennedy, Rougvie, Cooper, McLeish, Miller, Strachan (McMaster), Bell, McGhee (Black), Hewitt, Weir.

Fourth round — Aberdeen 1 (Hewitt), Celtic 0.
Leighton; Kennedy, Rougvie, McMaster, McLeish, Miller, Strachan, Simpson (Bell), McGhee, Hewitt, Weir.

Quarter-final — Aberdeen 4 (McGhee, Simpson, Strachan 2 pens), Kilmarnock 2.
Leighton; Kennedy, Hamilton, McMaster, McLeish, Miller, Strachan (Watson), Cooper, McGhee, Simpson, Hewitt.

Semi-final — St Mirren 1, Aberdeen 1 (Strachan pen).
Leighton; Kennedy, Rougvie (Bell), McMaster, McLeish, Miller, Strachan, Cooper, McGhee, Simpson, Hewitt.

Replay — St Mirren 2, Aberdeen 3 (McGhee, Simpson, Weir).
Leighton; Rougvie, McMaster, Cooper, McLeish, Miller, Strachan, Simpson, McGhee, Hewitt, Weir (Watson).

Final — Rangers 1, Aberdeen 4 (McLeish, McGhee, Strachan, Cooper). After extra time.
Leighton; Kennedy, Rougvie, McMaster (Bell), McLeish, Miller, Strachan, Cooper, McGhee, Simpson, Hewitt (Black).

1983

Third round — Hibs 1, Aberdeen 4 (Weir, Simpson, Watson, McGhee).
Leighton; Kennedy, Rougvie, McMaster (Watson), McLeish, Miller, Black, Simpson, McGhee, Bell, Weir.

Fourth round — Aberdeen 1 (Simpson), Dundee 0.
Leighton; Kennedy, Rougvie, Cooper, McLeish, Miller, Black, Simpson, McGhee, Bell, Weir.

Quarter-final — Partick Thistle 1, Aberdeen 2 (Cooper, Weir).
Leighton; Kennedy, Rougvie, Cooper, McLeish, Miller, Strachan, Simpson, McGhee, Bell (Black), Weir.

Semi-final — Celtic 0, Aberdeen 1 (Weir).
Leighton; Kennedy, Rougvie, Cooper (Weir), McLeish, Miller, Strachan, Simpson, McGhee, Bell, Black (Watson).

Final — Rangers 0, Aberdeen 1 (Black). After extra time.
Leighton; Rougvie (Watson), McMaster, Cooper, McLeish, Miller, Strachan, Simpson, McGhee, Black, Weir (Hewitt).

1984

Third round — Aberdeen 1 (Weir), Kilmarnock 1.
Leighton; McKimmie, Rougvie, McMaster (Porteous), McLeish, Miller, Strachan, Black, McGhee, Hewitt (Cooper), Weir.

Replay — Kilmarnock 1, Aberdeen 3 (Strachan, Miller, Weir).
Leighton; McKimmie, Rougvie (Hewitt), Cooper, McLeish, Miller, Strachan (Porteous), Black, McGhee, Angus, Weir.

Fourth round — Clyde 0, Aberdeen 2 (Angus, Cooper).
Leighton; McKimmie (McMaster), Rougvie, Cooper, McLeish, Miller, Strachan, Black, McGhee (Hewitt), Angus, Weir.

Quarter-final — Aberdeen 0, Dundee United 0.
Leighton; McKimmie, Rougvie, Cooper, McLeish, Miller, Strachan (Hewitt), Black, McGhee, Simpson, Angus.

Replay — Dundee United 0, Aberdeen 1 (McGhee).
Leighton; McKimmie, Rougvie (Mitchell), Cooper, McLeish, Miller, Strachan, Simpson, McGhee, Black, Angus.

Semi-final — Dundee 0, Aberdeen 2 (Porteous, Strachan).
Leighton; Mitchell, Rougvie, Simpson, McLeish, Miller, Strachan, Black, Porteous (Bell), Angus, Hewitt (Cowan).

Final — Celtic 1, Aberdeen 2 (Black, McGhee). After extra time.
Leighton; McKimmie, Rougvie (Stark), Cooper, McLeish, Miller, Strachan, Simpson, McGhee, Black, Weir (Bell).

1986

Third-round — Aberdeen 4 (Stark, Miller, McDougall, McLeish), Montrose 1.
Leighton; McKimmie, McQueen, Stark, McLeish, Miller, Black, Simpson, McDougall, Bett, Weir (Porteous).

Fourth round — Arbroath 0, Aberdeen 1 (J. Miller).
Leighton; Cooper, McQueen, Bett, McLeish, W. Miller, Black, Simpson, McDougall, Angus, J. Miller.

Quarter-final — Dundee 2, Aberdeen 2 (Hewitt 2).
Leighton; McKimmie, Angus, Cooper, McLeish, Miller, Black, Simpson (Stark), Hewitt, Bett, Weir (Wright).

Replay — Aberdeen 2 (Black, Weir), Dundee 1. After extra time.
Leighton; Cooper, McKimmie, Stark (Angus), McLeish, Miller, Black (Wright), Simpson, Hewitt, Bett, Weir.

Semi-final — Hibs 0, Aberdeen 3 (Stark, Black, J. Miller).
Gunn; McKimmie, Angus, Stark (McMaster), McLeish, W. Miller, Black, Cooper (J. Miller), McDougall, Bett, Hewitt.

Final — Hearts 0, Aberdeen 3 (Hewitt 2, Stark).
Leighton; McKimmie, McQueen, McMaster (Stark), McLeish, W. Miller, Hewitt (J. Miller), Cooper, McDougall, Bett, Weir.

Scottish League Cup

Season 1955/56

Qualifying section

Hibs 0, Aberdeen 1 (Buckley); Aberdeen 3 (Mulhall, Leggat, Yorston), Dunfermline 2; Aberdeen 3 (Wishart, Glen pen, Buckley), Clyde 2; Aberdeen 2 (Buckley, O'Neill), Hibs 1; Dunfermline 2, Aberdeen 2 (Buckley 2); Clyde 1, Aberdeen 2 (Leggat 2).

Quarter-final — first leg — Aberdeen 5 (Leggat 3, Buckley 2), Hearts 3.

Second leg — Hearts 2, Aberdeen 4 (Yorston, Leggat, Hather 2).

Semi-final — Rangers 1, Aberdeen 2 (Leggat, Wishart).
Martin; Paterson, Mitchell, Wilson, Clunie, Glen, Leggat, Yorston, Buckley, Wishart, Hather.

Final — St Mirren 1, Aberdeen 2 (own goal, Leggat).
Martin; Mitchell, Caldwell, Wilson, Clunie, Glen, Leggat, Yorston, Buckley, Wishart, Hather.

Season 1976/77

Qualifying section

Aberdeen 2 (Harper, Graham), Kilmarnock 0; Aberdeen 1 (Harper, pen), Ayr 0; Aberdeen 4 (Harper 2, Williamson 2), St Mirren 0; Ayr 1, Aberdeen 1 (Harper); Kilmarnock 2, Aberdeen 1 (Harper).

Quarter-final — first leg — Aberdeen 1 (Harper), Stirling Albion 0.

Second leg — Stirling Albion 1, Aberdeen 0. After extra time.

Replay — Stirling Albion 0, Aberdeen 2 (Scott, Smith).

Semi-final — Rangers 1, Aberdeen 5 (Scott 3, Harper, Jarvie).
Clark; Kennedy, Williamson, Smith (Thomson), Garner, Miller, Sullivan, Scott, Harper, Jarvie, Graham.

Final — Celtic 1, Aberdeen 2 (Jarvie, Robb). After extra time.
Clark; Kennedy, Williamson, Smith, Garner, Miller, Sullivan, Scott, Harper, Jarvie (Robb), Graham.

Skol Cup/League Cup

Season 1985-86

Second round — Aberdeen 5 (Stark, McQueen pen, McDougall 2) Ayr 0.

Third round — St Johnstone 0, Aberdeen 2 (Hewitt, McDougall).

Quarter-final — Aberdeen 1 (Black), Hearts 0.

Semi-final — first leg — Dundee United 0, Aberdeen 1 (Weir). Leighton; McKimmie, Mitchell, Stark, McLeish, Miller, Black, Simpson (Gray), McDougall (Falconer), Cooper, Hewitt.

Second leg — Aberdeen 1 (McDougall), Dundee United 0. Leighton; McKimmie, Mitchell, Stark (Gray), McLeish, Miller, Angus, Simpson, McDougall, Cooper, Hewitt.

Final — Hibs 0, Aberdeen 3 (Black 2, Stark). Leighton; McKimmie, Mitchell, Stark, McLeish, Miller, Black (Gray), Simpson, McDougall, Cooper, Hewitt.

Southern League Cup
Season 1945/46

Qualifying round — Kilmarnock 1, Aberdeen 1 (Williams); Aberdeen 4 (Baird 2, Kiddie, Williams), Hibs 1; Aberdeen 2 (Hamilton 2), Partick Thistle 1; Aberdeen 1 (Williams), Kilmarnock 0; Hibs 3, Aberdeen 2 (Baird, Cowie); Partick Thistle 0, Aberdeen 0.

Quarter-final — Aberdeen 2 (Williams, Hamilton), Ayr 0.

Semi-final — Aberdeen 2 (Baird, Williams), Airdrie 2.

Replay — Aberdeen 5 (Strauss, Kiddie 2, Williams, Baird pen), Airdrie 3.

Final — Aberdeen 3 (Baird, Williams, Taylor), Rangers 2. Johnstone; Cooper, McKenna, Cowie, Dunlop, Taylor, Kiddie, Hamilton, Williams, Baird, McCall.

Drybrough Cup
Season 1971/72

First round — East Fife 0, Aberdeen 3 (G. Buchan, Harper, Graham).

Semi-final — Airdrie 1, Aberdeen 4 (own goal, G. Buchan, Willoughby, Robb).

Final — Aberdeen 2 (Robb, Harper pen), Celtic 1.

1980/81

First round — Aberdeen 4 (Scanlon 3, Watson), Airdrie 1.

Semi-final — Morton 2, Aberdeen 4 (Scanlon 2, Strachan pen, McGhee).

Final — Aberdeen 2 (Jarvie, Cowan), St Mirren 1.

CHAMPIONSHIP SUCCESSES

Scottish League Division A — 1954/55

Played 30; won 24; drawn 1; lost 5; for 73; against 26; points 49.

Players and appearances — Glen 30, Hather 30, Young 30, Mitchell 29, Buckley 28, Yorston 28, Martin 27, Leggat 26, W. Smith 25, Wishart 23, Allister 21, O'Neil 12, Wallace 5, Caldwell 5, Hamilton 4, Brown 3, Morrison 3, Paterson 1.

Premier League

1979/80

Played 36; won 19; drawn 10; lost 7; for 68; against 36; points 48.

Clark 35, Kennedy 35, McLeish 35, Archibald 34, Strachan 33, McMaster 32 (plus 2 as a substitute), Miller 31, Scanlon 25 (4), Jarvie 22 (8), Rougvie 22 (3), Garner 20, McGhee 15 (6), Considine 14, Watson 12 (5), Hamilton 11 (2), Harper 8 (3), Bell 4 (6), Davidson 2 (5), Sullivan 2 (3), Hewitt 2 (2), Neale Cooper 1, Leighton 1.

1983/84

Played 36; won 25; drawn 7; lost 4; for 78; against 21; points 57.

Leighton 36, Rougvie 35, Miller 34, McLeish 32, McGhee 30 (3), Weir 26 (1), Cooper 25 (1), Strachan 24 (1), Hewitt 22 (11), Bell 21 (3), McKimmie 17 (1), Black 14 (4), Stark 11 (3), McMaster 11 (1), Angus 9 (3), McIntyre 7 (4), Mitchell 6 (3), Porteous 5 (9), Cowan 5, Falconer 4 (5), Robertson 1, Wright (1).

1984/85

Played 36; won 27; drawn 5; lost 4; for 89; against 26; points 59.

Leighton 34, W. Miller 34, McKimmie 34, McQueen 33 (2), Simpson 33, Stark 30 (2), McLeish 30, McDougall 27 (1), Black 27, Angus 21 (7), Bell 18 (4), Cooper 17 (3), Weir 15 (1), Hewitt 11 (10), Falconer 10 (6), Mitchell 7 (7), Porteous 7 (6), Cowan 6 (10), Gunn 2, J. Miller (1), McMaster (1).